I testify that one cannot come to full faith in this latter-day work—and thereby find the fullest measure of peace and comfort in these, our times—until he or she embraces the divinity of the Book of Mormon and the Lord Jesus Christ, of whom it testifies.

Jeffrey R. Holland

From the HEART

CHARITY IN THE BOOK OF MORMON

MARILYN ARNOLD

CFI
SPRINGVILLE, UTAH

This is not an official publication of The Church of Jesus Christ of Latter-day Saints. The opinions and views expressed herein belong solely to the author and do not necessarily represent the opinions or views of Cedar Fort, Inc. Permission for the use of sources, graphics, and photos is also solely the responsibility of the author.

ISBN 13: 978–1–59955–485–3

Published by CFI, an imprint of Cedar Fort, Inc., 2373 W. 700 S., Springville, UT 84663
Distributed by Cedar Fort, Inc., www.cedarfort.com

LIBRARY OF CONGRESS CATALOGING-IN-PUBLICATION DATA

Arnold, Marilyn, 1935-
  From the heart : charity in the Book of Mormon / Marilyn Arnold.
    p. cm.
  ISBN 978-1-59955-485-3
  1. Book of Mormon--Criticism, interpretation, etc. 2. Love--Religious
aspects--Church of Jesus Christ of Latter-day Saints. 3. Charity--Mormon
authors. 4. Church of Jesus Christ of Latter-day Saints--Doctrines. I.
Title.

  BX8627.A74 2011
  241'.4--dc22

        2010035565

Cover design by Danie Romrell
Cover design © 2011 by Lyle Mortimer
Edited and typeset by Heidi Doxey

Page i quote: Jeffrey R. Holland, "Safety for the Soul," *Ensign*, Nov. 2009, 89–90.

Printed in the United States of America

10 9 8 7 6 5 4 3 2 1

Printed on acid-free paper

To the Relief Society sisters who have celebrated
the Book of Mormon with me.

ADDITIONAL WORKS
BY MARILYN ARNOLD

FICTION

Unidentified Lying Objects
Perfecting Amiable
Minding Mama
The Classmates
Fields of Clover
Sky Full of Ribbons
Song of Hope
Desert Song

NONFICTION

Bittersweet: A Daughter's Memoir
Sacred Hymns of the Book of Mormon
Pure Love: Readings on Sixteen Enduring Virtues
Sweet Is the Word: Reflections on the Book of Mormon
Willa Cather: A Reference Guide
Willa Cather's Short Fiction

EDITOR

Book of Mormon Reference Companion
A Chorus for Peace: A Global Anthology of Poetry by Women
A Reader's Companion to the Fiction of Willa Cather

Contents

PART TWO

MOMENTS OF GRACE, CHRIST'S LOVE
SHOWERED ON EARTH

PART THREE

CLIMACTIC EVENTS

A *Prophet*
SPEAKS . . .

It is not just that the Book of Mormon teaches us truth, though it indeed does that. It is not just that the Book of Mormon bears testimony of Christ, though it indeed does that, too. But there is something more. There is a power in the book which will begin to flow into your lives the moment you begin a serious study of the book. You will find greater power to resist temptation. You will find the power to avoid deception. You will find the power to stay on the strait and narrow path. The scriptures are called "the words of life" (D&C 84:85), and nowhere is that more true than it is of the Book of Mormon. When you begin to hunger and thirst after those words, you will find life in greater and greater abundance.

—Ezra Taft Benson[1]

It is the power President Benson describes that I have discovered, and the hunger for the words of this incredible book, the Book of Mormon, that drives me to write again about it. You, too, can feel that spiritual power, that life-enhancing hunger for the truths contained in its pages. You, too, can be filled as you join me on this latest journey. This new volume comes right from my heart. And, what is more important, it comes from the hearts of men anciently who kept the record and from the heart of Joseph Smith, who translated the record through the Spirit and love of God.

---

1. Ezra Taft Benson, "The Book of Mormon—Keystone of Our Religion," *Ensign*, Nov. 1986, 7.

PREFACE

MY *Letter* TO THE *World*

A unique and wonderful poet, Emily Dickinson, began one of her poems with these words: "This is my letter to the World / That never wrote to Me—".[1] I am quite certain that she was speaking of the body of her work, most of which was not published in her lifetime. She was one who became rather reclusive as she matured, but who nonetheless experienced life's pains, joys, and contradictions with rare poignancy and understanding. She painstakingly composed her many hundreds of poems not knowing if anyone outside a few chosen confidants would ever see more than a few of them. But she had to write them. She had to say what she knew and, yes, what she didn't know.

For the record, I am happy to claim fellowship with the believing, with the yea-sayers who answer to a feeling deep inside, to an undeniable testimony of the soul that bears witness to what prophets ancient and modern have proclaimed—that God lives, that he speaks through a prophet today, that he has restored the gospel taught by Jesus Christ in its fulness, that the Book of Mormon is the truest book ever published, and that God chose Joseph Smith in premortal life to be the agent of its restoration in latter times. This is my letter to the world that never wrote to me either. Move over, Emily Dickinson—you have company.

---

1. Emily Dickinson, untitled poem, "This is my letter to the world." *The Complete Poems of Emily Dickinson*, ed. Thomas H. Johnson (Boston: Little, Brown and Co., 1960), 211. This poem is widely anthologized and available online.

Despite a rigorous education in one of the country's finest graduate schools, in matters of ultimate importance I am a classic case of a slow learner. Since childhood I had believed The Church of Jesus Christ of Latter-day Saints (the "Mormon" Church) to be the only organization on earth to be blessed with Christ's gospel in its fulness. I had *believed* it, but I hadn't *known* it as I know it now, with every fiber of my being. I ache when I hear of someone who was reared in the Church drifting away, choosing the ease of non-commitment, of undemanding half belief or unbelief—or worse still, becoming an enemy to the Church and going public with his or her disaffection. I ache because this person could have been spared the agony that sometimes accompanies intentional separation, spared by honest, prayerful study of the Book of Mormon.

It also frightens me just a little to wonder if at some point I, too, might have been vulnerable to the siren call of worldly disdain for revealed truth and living prophets. Might I, too, have been talked out of my faith at some point, or might I have talked myself out of my faith? How grateful I am to have made the decision a good number of years ago to do whatever it took to move beyond habit and somewhat complacent—though fully accepting—belief to sure knowledge.

I had gone along for many extremely busy years, absorbed in schooling and career, and at the same time serving in a variety of Church assignments, many of them on curriculum committees charged with preparing lesson manuals for Church auxiliaries. I was so busy, in fact, that I had never made an intense, concentrated study of the Book of Mormon. Reading it obediently, often piecemeal, was one thing; studying it from cover to cover, again and again, with energy and pleading prayer, was quite another. Then one night as I was preparing for bed— it was late, it was always late—I turned on the tiny black and white, antenna-garnished television set in my bathroom. In those days I had no time for television except late at night as I was unwinding before climbing into bed. As it happened, that night KBYU-TV was rebroadcasting President Ezra Taft Benson's recent birthday celebration.

Just as the picture came on the screen, President Benson entered slowly from the right. At that moment, to my complete surprise, the Spirit told me plainly that he was a prophet of God. Tears came to my eyes. It was the most unlikely of moments—I was running bath water—and yet the message was loud and clear. Ezra Taft Benson was the Lord's chosen servant, his vessel for dispensing God's word and will at that time.

In bed that night the import of what had happened struck me forcefully. What had President Benson been stressing throughout his ministry? Read and study the Book of Mormon. Cease to neglect that divine gift and take it into your mind and heart. It was a moment of awakening for me, a moment of realizing that despite significant time and effort spent in Church service, I had not made the Book of Mormon truly mine. With that troubling realization, I drifted into a somewhat restless sleep.

The next day, which I think was a Friday, professional work totally absorbed me, as it always did. I came home exhausted that evening, as I always did. Whether I went for a run or not, I can't recall; but if there was daylight, I liked to run between day work and night study and writing, to clear my mind. (In deference to my aging and long abused knees, I now walk rather than run.) What I do remember is that I began a reassessment of my life at that time, an exercise long overdue. It struck me like a guided missile that I had spent a good share of my professional life studying, teaching, and writing about the world's literature. And all the time, there on my shelf was the Book of Mormon, possibly the most important book ever published, read only dutifully over the years. Don't ask me why. I wonder at my younger self still. How could I have let it go like that?

Then another thought hit me. My academic training, which was long and rigorous, was in the study of the written word. I had learned how to read and understand literary texts—narratives, essays, poetry, journals, drama. And what was the Book of Mormon but literature of the highest caliber, literature from the mind of the Lord, recorded through his chosen servants. And in English, translated only once and that directly from the Lord. Here was narrative, poetry, prose non-fiction, inspired personal reflection, and drama of the first order. And what had I done with that training? Well, I had taught lovely young people how to appreciate good literature and how to craft a sentence, a worthwhile endeavor, surely; and I had written for the Church. But beyond that, I had focused on wholesome literary texts—publishing books and articles, delivering lectures and papers at forums and conferences, organizing symposia, editing literary journals, and so on.

I knew then, with a surety I had rarely experienced before, that it was time to turn those years of education and experience to serving something beyond my professional career. Something of greater importance. Something of eternal consequence. I knew it was time to apply my training to a more specific kind of service in the kingdom, something that reached beyond the worldly concerns of academia, else why was I blessed to receive such training? I knew it was time to study the Book of Mormon with, at the very least, the same intensity that I had devoted to the study of literary texts and lives. I also knew it was time to raise my life to a higher spiritual plane, to cast off anything superficial or incompatible with pure pursuit of divine truth in the Book of Mormon. In a word, I began to desire sanctification with my whole being, to be worthy of the guidance of the Spirit in my study.

I began studying, devouring the Book of Mormon daily, poring over every word and phrase. As I read the early chapters, I was overwhelmed with a desire to write about the book. I came to want that more ardently than I had ever wanted anything. As I prayed fervently for permission and understanding and the ability to write about this sacred text, I spent a long night on my knees, weeping and praying for forgiveness and guidance. The Spirit led me to a passage in the Doctrine and Covenants that I will never forget. It seemed to speak to me directly. It was in Section 11. The Lord is speaking through Joseph Smith to Joseph's brother Hyrum, who had expressed a desire to preach the gospel. Hyrum is counseled to prepare thoroughly through study before attempting to preach and was told that when the time was ripe, he would be allowed to teach. Verse 21 seemed to speak directly to me that night:

> Seek not to declare my word, but first seek to obtain my word, and then shall your tongue be loosed; then, if you desire, you shall have my Spirit and my word, yea, the power of God unto the convincing of men.

I was then prompted to revisit my patriarchal blessing, which I hadn't done in some time. And there they were, words I had not remembered at all, words that were amazing echoes of D&C 11:21. And there also was a statement that I would teach the gospel "by the pen," in other words, by writing. At the end of that experience I knew the Book of Mormon was the key to my testimony, and I began from that day to study it with a determination to write about it. Writing the book that had its genesis in that first night of soul-searching and divine guidance was a life-altering experience.[2]

I was thirteen or fourteen at the time I received my patriarchal blessing. What did I know about such things at that age? People of my generation remember—and regret—that the gospel was not taught to youngsters in the Church as it is now. We did not study the scriptures, as *scripture*, in Primary, Sunday School, and MIA. Even seminary classes did not stir my fires as they should have (admittedly, my fault). Like many others, especially those who did not serve formal missions in youth—and that includes the majority of women—I have had to make up the difference in maturity. A late bloomer, I was, oh yes, but I'm here to tell you that I did bloom. And it was studying and writing about the Book of Mormon through the unmistakable guidance of the Spirit that brought me to flower in the gospel. Even now I weep to think of it, so deep is my gratitude. Living daily with the Book of Mormon, and writing about it, changed me forever. How grateful I am for that change, that blessed transformation. I promise that it can happen to you and to anyone who truly seeks to know.

I will never be famous for staying in the Church and growing mightily in the faith, but I feel some urgency just now to stand up and be counted, to publish my "letter to the world." I also feel some urgency to reach out to those who have chosen to leave, or others who have chosen to stay despite their uncertain faith, or still others who have chosen not to become familiar with the Church and its doctrines. And yes, I speak to those firm in the faith who nonetheless have not yet been overwhelmed by the miracle of the Book of Mormon. (Fear not, stalwarts, I gladly welcome you who know the book and love it as I do. We can relish it yet one more time together.)

Why do I focus specifically on the Book of Mormon again? Because, as I have indicated, that remarkable book changed my heart and my life forever. It grows more precious with each passing day. Over the years,

---

2. The book is titled *Sweet Is the Word: Reflections on The Book of Mormon—Its Narrative, Teachings, and People* (American Fork: Covenant, 1996). More recently, my inner fires were stirred to write poems inspired by the Book of Mormon, poems then set to lovely music by Maurine Ozment, with Lisa Farr's invaluable assistance. The book's title is *Sacred Hymns of the Book of Mormon* (Springville: Cedar Fort, 2009).

the Church has given me much, but if it had given me nothing but the Book of Mormon, that would be enough. To all of you, in the Church or not, I reach out in earnest pleading and say you owe it to yourselves to come to the Book of Mormon with a mind and heart honestly seeking to know if this book is what it claims to be—an inspired record of ancient covenant peoples who left Jerusalem and settled in the western hemisphere many centuries ago, an inspired record of the prophecies, doctrines, and ultimately the personal ministry of Jesus Christ in the New World. I now understand something of what prompted the Nephite prophet Alma to cry,

> O that I were an angel, and could have the wish of mine heart,
> that I might go forth and speak with the trump of God, with a voice
> to shake the earth, . . .
> Yea, I would declare unto every soul, as with the voice of thunder, repentance and the plan of redemption, that they should repent
> and come unto our God, that there might not be more sorrow upon
> all the face of the earth.

And then, Alma seems to catch himself and apologize for his grandiose desire:

> But behold, I am a man, and do sin in my wish; for I ought to
> be content with the things which the Lord hath allotted unto me.
> (Alma 29:1–3)

And so must I be content, for the Lord has allotted to me to write.

Perhaps Alma's words take on even more significance when we realize that as a young man he sought to destroy the church. But the Lord had a work for him to perform, as he had for Saul of Tarsus, and he sent an angel to set Alma straight. The young man's conversion was certainly more dramatic than mine, but it was no more complete and lasting than mine. I am still so impassioned by the Book of Mormon, so in love with its doctrine, its language, its people, its truth—with the whole of the Savior's gospel—that I want to shout my joy from the housetops. And with that sure testimony of the book's authenticity has come an unshakable testimony of Joseph Smith, The Church of Jesus Christ of Latter-day Saints, and all its prophets from Joseph to the present. I wish I could convince everyone on earth to know as I know and to believe as I believe.

What is a mere mortal (and a non-prophet at that!) to do with such a herculean desire? Modern-day Church leaders whom I count as friends have suggested that I can reach more people through writing than through any other means, and so I write this book, my letter to the world. My heartfelt invitation to humankind to be, as the Savior urged, "believing." Come, read the Book of Mormon—more than that, study it, devour it, pray about it, make it yours.

What I hope to do in this current volume is share a few ideas that have stirred my mind and shaken my very soul in my most recent readings of the Book of Mormon. Truly, certain passages and events have fairly leaped off the page and said, "Pay heed, this book is for you." Maybe they will strike you as they have me, with the power President Benson spoke of. If not, perhaps they can nonetheless suggest to you a new way of coming to this sacred book and encourage you to find your own new ways. How can I presume to do this, you might ask, since I am neither a scholar of religious studies, nor a certified teacher of scriptural works.

I will not rehearse here the multitude of impressive, scholarly arguments and proofs for the book's authenticity, and there are many. The voluminous writings of the late Hugh Nibley are a case in point. Many others, all wiser heads than mine, have discovered ancient Hebrew poetic forms such as chiasmus throughout the Book of Mormon; they have charted word prints that prove multiple authorship, they have found cultural, historical, geographical, archaeological, and geological correspondences in the lands of Egypt and Mesoamerica; and they are still making important discoveries.

The only observable skills I bring to the task are those I have already mentioned. But in reading and assessing hundreds of literary texts, and writing a good many of my own, I think I have learned to distinguish between a written discourse that is genuine and valuable, and one that is spurious and worthless, or somewhere in between. In short, I have come to know genius and truth and grandeur when I encounter them, just as I know ignorance and posturing and trash. More than that, perhaps, I have found new ways of knowing and feeling.

The Book of Mormon speaks to the part of me that recognizes beauty and wonder in its use of language, and intelligence and truth in what it says; it speaks to my mind. It also speaks to the part of me that apprehends at the level of what Wordsworth called "thoughts that do often lie too deep for tears."[3] This is a level beyond intellectual analysis, beyond literary criticism, beyond formal argument, beyond scholarly training and experience. It is the level at which the Spirit speaks to my soul, and to every earnest, seeking soul. It is a knowing that cannot be tested by mortal instruments or scholarly reasoning, although the book certainly passes scrutiny in many tangible criteria. It is a knowing more precious than diamonds or rubies, more precious than life. It is a knowing that wipes away every inclination toward evil, that erases the desire for sin. It is a knowing that, were it universal, would eliminate poverty and hate and war. It is a knowing that opens the heart to the reality and love and joy of Jesus Christ, our Lord and Redeemer. It is also a knowing that leads to self-assessment, humility, repentance, and commitment to things higher than one's own success or gratification. It is a knowing that might well be what is meant by worship.

In short, the Book of Mormon is a miracle, precious beyond mortal means of assigning value. What I know is that the Book of Mormon I hold in my hands could not possibly have been the product of any mortal imagination—be the mortal scholar or fictionist—much less a meagerly educated farm boy of the early nineteenth century.

Most assuredly, the Book of Mormon is a stumbling block for some. Why do some discredit it unread? Why do some choose to ignore it? Why do some choose to think that it could not possibly be authentic? *An ancient record inscribed on metal plates buried for many hundreds of years? Spare me.* Of course, the fact that other early civilizations kept such records proves nothing and only confuses the mind already settled in negative territory. Some avoid reading the book for fear of discovering its veracity. I plead with you to approach the Book of Mormon with a mind open to the possibility that it is what it claims to be: a record inscribed, in the main, by a man named Mormon; a record that is in large part an abridgement of nearly a thousand years of history and doctrine lived and taught by immigrants to the Americas; and a record that begins more than 2600 years ago.

---

3. William Wordsworth, "Ode: Intimations of Immortality from Recollections of Early Childhood," Section XI, *Seven Centuries of Verse: English and American*, ed. A.J.M Smith (New York: Charles Scribner's Sons, 1967), 313. This poem is widely anthologized and available online.

But it is more than a history book, more than a book of narratives. It is a sacred book, written by holy men who "talk of Christ," who "rejoice in Christ," who "preach of Christ," and who "prophesy of Christ" (2 Nephi 25:26). And it was written mainly for our day by men who foresaw the annihilation of their own people and wrote that we might, as Moroni said, learn from their mistakes (see Mormon 9:31). That leaves the question: what of those who have left The Church of Jesus Christ of Latter-day Saints, and see their leaving that body as a freeing change? After all, the Church asks a great deal of its members. (And maybe that is one reason why so many love it unfailingly! They feel needed and inspired, part of a vibrant, wholesome, caring, serving community.)

We might well listen to British writer D.H. Lawrence who observed that Americans can be quite wrong in their notion of freedom. Freedom, he argues, does not come from "straying and breaking away" from places of heritage and commitment. Rather, he says, "Men are free when they are obeying some deep, inward voice of religious belief. Obeying from within. Men are free when they belong to a living, organic, believing community, active in fulfilling some unfulfilled, perhaps unrealized purpose." Further, he says, "Men are not free when they are doing just what they like. The moment you can do just what you like, there is nothing you care about doing."[4]

And so, I invite one and all to join me in a journey I feel compelled to make, a freeing excursion into the world of a book of scripture that is capable of changing today's world, one heart at a time. See the Book of Mormon for what it is. Do not judge it unread or read it with a closed mind. Surely, this magnificent scriptural record, translated through direct revelation, from what Moroni terms "reformed Egyptian," in little more than sixty working days, and containing the fulness of the everlasting gospel of Jesus Christ, would not have been given to and brought forth by anyone other than God's chosen prophet.

Isaiah (and others, their writings since lost from the Old Testament as we have it today) foresaw its coming. Chapter 29 of Isaiah testifies to the latter-day emergence from "the dust" of a sacred record kept by ancient prophets in a new land and buried in the ground (see also

---

4. D. H. Lawrence, "The Spirit of Place," *Studies in Classic American Literature* (New York: Viking Press, 1964, originally published by Thomas Seltzer, Inc.), 6.

2 Nephi 27). These early prophets knew that the record to be kept in a new land, specifically by descendants of Joseph of Egypt, would usher in the restoration of all sacred covenants, authority, and ordinances that over the centuries had been abandoned or altered through apostasy. Joseph Smith was the new vessel the Lord chose to carry the new message of divine hope and purpose. Of that truth, I bear solemn witness.

Perhaps now it is time to *show* rather than merely *tell* the captivating power of this magnificent book, let it speak for itself as it testifies of Christ and teaches us the kind of people we can become and must become. It also warns us, in no uncertain terms, of the dangers inherent in the self-centered, prideful, uncommitted life—in the life that lacks charity in the terms by which Paul (and Mormon) describe it.

Come, plunge with me into the book and let it have its way with you. Let it speak to you directly, heart to heart. Recognize how real its people are, and see in their failures lessons for your own success. See also in their glorious spiritual transformations, their lovely rebirths as children of Christ, the possibilities for yourself. The Book of Mormon is not unreachable. It is there to be discovered and loved by anyone willing to study it prayerfully with an honest desire to know if it is true. It has the power to change you in remarkable ways, splendid ways, eternal ways.

PART ONE

Charity, THE Greatest OF THESE

Prologue

How well I remember President Ezra Taft Benson's powerful admonitions, more than two decades ago, against falling into the sin of pride—"the universal sin, the great vice." He told us in a general conference address that "one of the major messages of the Book of Mormon" is "the sin of pride," and that the Book stands as a warning to us against becoming a prideful people. He also said that "the antidote for pride is humility—meekness, submissiveness. It is the broken heart and contrite spirit" (April 1989). Our recollection of his repeated references to the manifestations of pride in the Book of Mormon, and in modern society, may lead us to forget that President Benson spoke fervently not only about the danger and evil of pride, but also about the wondrous, saving goodness of charity. In successive April general conferences (1988 and 1989), he addressed first one, then the other. In October 1986, he had also spoken eloquently on charity. It seems the two subjects had been on his mind, one the reverse of the other. And they have been on my mind since my last intensive reading of the Book of Mormon.

As I closed the book yet again, with Mormon and Moroni, I was especially touched by their words to us, to me. Many times I was moved to tears, feeling deeply the immeasurable grief these men suffered. I also wept in gratitude for their constancy and their message. More than ever before, in reading the last words of these loving, selfless, and dear men, I felt an urgency to become less prideful and self-centered, to become a person of true charity, more worthy of their sacrifice and of the God they served to the end. How clearly I began to see that charity, which both Paul and Mormon describe in terms of self-forgetfulness, humility, and submissiveness, is—as President Benson says—"the antidote for pride."[1] No wonder those two ancient prophets declare charity to be "the greatest" of mortal virtues, the greatest of God's gifts to humankind. Charity then, in all its expressions, is my principal subject. And the Book of Mormon is my text. It was also President Ezra Taft Benson's text on at least two occasions:

> The final and crowning virtue of the divine character is charity, or the pure love of Christ (see Moroni 7:47). If we would truly seek to be more like our Savior and Master, then learning to love as He loves should be our highest goal. Mormon called charity "the greatest of all" (Moroni 7:46).
>
> . . . Charity never seeks selfish gratification. The pure love of Christ seeks only the eternal growth and joy of others.[2]

> It is the pure love of Christ, called charity, that the Book of Mormon testifies is the greatest of all—that never faileth, that endureth forever, that all men should have, and that without which they are nothing.[3]

❧

As I pondered Mormon's list of the attributes of charity (see Moroni 7:44–48, especially v. 45), I turned to Paul (1 Corinthians 13) whose list is echoed in Mormon. Both men speak of faith, hope, and charity; both say that charity is "the greatest of these," attesting that "charity never faileth." They have led me to ask, "Why is charity 'the greatest of these,' and especially, why greater than either faith or hope?"

In the Church we speak often of the importance of faith. We are rightly and repeatedly encouraged and admonished to seek faith in our Lord Jesus Christ and to act on that faith. It is the first principle of the gospel identified by Joseph Smith in what is often considered to be the creed of the Church, the Articles of Faith. No one could dispute its doctrinal prominence or significance. Given the importance

---

1. Ezra Taft Benson, "Beware of Pride," *Ensign*, May 1989, 4–7.
2. Ezra Taft Benson, "The Godly Characteristics of the Master," *Ensign*, Nov. 1986, 47.
3. Ezra Taft Benson. "The Great Commandment—Love the Lord," *Ensign*, May, 1988, 4.

of faith—and hope, too—why would these inspired ancient prophets, from two different eras and different lands on opposite sides of the world, insist that *charity* is the greatest attribute for which a mortal can and must strive? And they are not alone, for Nephi had said earlier that unless we have charity we are nothing (2 Nephi 26:30). Other Book of Mormon prophets teach the principle, too, whether they call it by name or describe it in other terms.

Living prophets are also teaching the doctrine of charity, of pure love, with sincerity and fervor. As I write this paragraph, I have just witnessed five sessions of the 179th Semi-annual Conference of The Church of Jesus Christ of Latter-day Saints. In address after address, apostles and prophets of the restored Church spoke movingly on this very subject. Chosen women leaders have done likewise, confirming in my mind and heart the importance of this subject *now*.

I was also grateful to see a lesson on charity in the Relief Society and Priesthood manual devoted to the teachings of Joseph Smith. Traditionally, even though Priesthood organizations are much involved in acts of service, we have regularly associated the concept of charity mainly with the Relief Society. Its very name seems to define its purpose: to provide "relief," usually of a domestic sort. Indeed, taking a casserole to a bereaved family is an act of charity, of love, and we come closer to understanding charity when we speak of that selfless act in those terms.

But in adopting for its motto the three-word phrase I cited from both Paul and Mormon, the Relief Society has proclaimed a broader, even loftier purpose than "relief" in the usual sense of the term: "Charity never faileth" (1 Corinthians 13:8; Moroni 7:46). Perhaps that is why charity is the greatest of gifts, because, although we can fail to exercise it, charity itself never, ever fails. It is always a positive thing; it is always beneficial. In considering such an amazing concept, we must realize that Paul and Mormon (and the Lord who gave them voice) do not speak of charity in a limited sense. In defining the term, they use synonyms descriptive of a life purpose that applies to all mortals—to become persons of charity in the fullest meaning of the word, to overcome every prideful impulse and habit of character.

Another answer to the question, "Why is charity 'the greatest of these'?" occurs to me. Charity is the loftiest attribute toward which mortals can aspire because if fully lived, it is the essence of the *consecrated life.* Faith and hope lead to charity, and they are necessary steps, but it is consecration that opens us to receive and give the pure love of Christ. The terms with which Paul and Mormon define charity all suggest consecration or the surrender of self in emulating the character of Christ.

This is not an easy concept to grasp, much less to live every day. We seem to have been born with sizable egos. Probably these are meant as protective devices to send us into the world with some ability to fend for ourselves. But I think we may have developed those egos at the expense of other, more godlike, traits. And certainly, advertisers have played to the ego by telling us that we "deserve" whatever they are selling, that we should pamper ourselves and indulge endlessly in worldly goods and pleasures. What if we really *wanted* to consecrate ourselves to the Lord and his Kingdom more than we wanted success, pleasure, or the things money can buy?

When we truly observe the Law of Consecration—and it is a *law*—we give ourselves to the Lord and his work. This is the ultimate expression of humility and charity. This is the losing of self that ultimately becomes the finding of one's Christlike self. And it is a voluntary choice. Throughout the Book of Mormon we see courageous mortals making that choice, giving up the world and consecrating themselves, never wavering, to lives of charity in the Lord's kingdom. In Part Two of this volume, we will rejoice together with these blessed people who stand as an exemplary counterbalance to the foolish and vain, to those caught in the deadly pride-suffering-humility-prosperity-pride cycle that marks the rises and falls in Nephite society. Sadly, the current of pride and hate in their fallen neighbors swept some of the consecrated and charitable off the planet, too. But there is a vast difference in the reward to which these faithful ones ascended.

THE *Last Words* OF THE *Last Prophets*

I

MORMON AND MORONI

I begin with the end, because the end was the beginning of my journey into new understanding of a book I have loved for many years, loved beyond any other book on earth. I begin with the two men who launched me into this latest journey of understanding: the last Nephite survivor, Moroni, and his father, Mormon, who was the principal abridger of the record we know as the Book of Mormon. This father and son witnessed the collapse of their own nation, a collapse that Mormon attributes specifically to pride (Moroni 8:27). Seeing that awful descent, these faithful men engraved words on metal plates, not only to preserve a priceless record—a feast of the words of Christ—but also to warn us against falling into the insidious pattern of selfish pridefulness that destroyed their people, both spiritually and physically.

We can learn much from the writings of these witnesses to the closing of an era, to the total loss of hundreds of thousands of people and all earthly things they had known. We must fully absorb their unwavering testimonies of Jesus Christ and come to know with our whole beings, as they did, that Jesus is the Son of God, the Redeemer of the world, and that their record is undeniably authentic and of ultimate consequence to our eternal souls. We must also read and take to heart their admonitions to us in our day. Fearing for us—Moroni has seen us in vision and knows our "doing" (Mormon 8:35)—Moroni and Mormon warn us against the character flaws and sins, the many manifestations of pride, that spelled destruction for the Nephites.

This faithful father and son were not the only ancient prophets to issue pointed warnings to our day as they spoke or closed their records. Studying their words has taken me back also to the first Nephi's closing words and those of his younger brother Jacob, and Jacob's son, Enos. The matters of pride and charity were on their minds, too, and they feared for us as well as for their own descendants.

For many years I have had a special feeling for Moroni, but with recent readings of the books of Ether, Mormon, and Moroni, the feeling has deepened and literally bowled me over. Mormon, too, has touched me more deeply than in previous readings. I think I know why. I experienced a heightened realization that these men truly were speaking directly to us, to you and me, and that they were admonishing us particularly in the matter of charity, the pure love of Christ. As I have said, these incredible men saw chosen peoples fail in charity, in all its forms—failures detailed in the record over the centuries—and they saw the terrible consequences of those failures. Unable to save their own people from such consequences, they can and do warn us. These prophets have moved me to both anguish and joy. I know them as mortal men, and I know them as oracles of God.

Moroni was the last surviving Nephite and final keeper of the record. Many people think of Moroni in connection with his challenge in Moroni 10:4 to read the Book of Mormon and then verify its truth by asking the Lord for confirmation through the Holy Ghost. Many also are aware of him as the angel who visited Joseph Smith and delivered a set of metal plates for translation, gold plates bearing ancient inscriptions. Others identify him mainly as the shiny figure atop Mormon temples, trumpeting the restoration of the gospel of Jesus Christ in modern times. Some confuse him with Captain Moroni, who preceded him by five hundred years or so, after whom he was named.

Moroni and Mormon are more than faceless names. They are men, foreordained in the heavens for their specific earthly assignments. That they were foreordained makes them no less real. They are not simply the products of someone's imagination, characters in a book, or persons of legend. They lived and breathed and fought and died. They also wrote.

If they are real, and if what they say is true, then the Book of Mormon is true—indisputably true. And if the Book of Mormon is true, the church through which it came forth is the church of the living God on earth. To read and come to know the words written by these men is to know the reality of their existence as men and the truth of their words.

I feel a brotherhood with Mormon and Moroni, a brotherhood deepened by awe and gratitude. In reverence, I try to comprehend their incomprehensible suffering. Both men kept the faith and recorded their testimonies through trials beyond mortal imagining, beyond human comfort or rescue. When a man like Mormon or Moroni watches his whole civilization crumble; when his people have sunk into every imaginable depravity, including cannibalism; when he witnesses the total annihilation of cities, people, family, and friends; but still he keeps the faith, then it is meet that we hear what he has to say. When everything he has known has perished, a man is not going to inscribe lies on metal plates that are meant to last through the ages after he buries them in the ground. Certainly, the last words of any upright man merit our thoughtful consideration, and none more than the words of this stalwart father and son.

In the end, with even his father gone, Moroni is left with no surviving spouse, children, parents, siblings, or friends. He has no home. The only other living mortals in his war-ravaged world are brutal, bloodthirsty enemies who would slaughter him in a moment and destroy the record if they found him. Is a man under these circumstances likely to make the perpetration of a gigantic hoax his major concern? For more than thirty years? And is a rural nineteenth century New England farm boy named Joseph Smith likely to invent such a record (of five hundred–plus printed pages!) and then suffer every imaginable abuse and deprivation, and ultimately death, in defense of his invention? Hardly.

Moroni's father, Mormon, was among the final twenty-four Nephite survivors of the last great war in Book of Mormon lands. He was, in fact, commander of the once-vast armies of his people. It hardly seems possible that Mormon also managed to lead the church and abridge the records of his people's thousand-year history into one book, which has been named after him. What a feat that was, carrying out that sacred work through the tumultuous years of war and anguish, years in which he also taught and prophesied as well as led armies and suffered countless wounds. Perhaps even more difficult than war and death were the atrocities he witnessed as his people became like wild beasts, bereft of feeling and hope, empty of faith and charity.

Moroni had a perspective that possibly went even beyond his father's. He not only experienced those final agonizing years of his people; he not only read the records in his care (he alludes to earlier writers); but he also added to them three of Mormon's personal discourses, writings Mormon had not included in his record. Thus we have one of Mormon's extremely important sermons and two of his letters to Moroni, his dear son. The sermon and first letter were written while the church was still functional, to some degree, though war erupted frequently and was always a threat. The second letter was written later, when the Nephite nation was on the verge of collapse, both morally and militarily.

Beyond inscribing a few of his father's writings into his own record, Moroni took up the record that the prophet Ether had made of an earlier civilization, one that began with a small group that left Jerusalem and later sailed to the New World at the time of the Tower of Babel and the confusing of tongues, ca. 2200 BC. That group has come to be called Jaredites, after an early leader. Lehi's company, comprised of his family and a few others, made the same journey in 600 BC. Mormon and Moroni were descendants of the first great Nephi, Lehi's middle son. The second group, however, were not aware of the earlier group until centuries later when some of their number came upon an enormous expanse of ruins and a record (see Omni 1:20–22; Mosiah 21:25–27).

It is telling that the Nephites called this area Land of Desolation. It stands as a solemn witness to the destruction of a once-great civilization, and it foreshadows the destruction of the Nephite nation. The explorers who happened on these ruins also met up with Coriantumr, the last Jaredite survivor other than Ether (see Omni 1:21–22). Moroni abridged the record of Ether and added it, with some of his own commentary and writings, to the record made largely by his father, Mormon. Moroni must have felt a real kinship with Ether and Coriantumr, all three of them last vestiges of fallen civilizations.

Thus, as I suggested, Moroni brings a unique perspective to the Book of Mormon. He lived with, and protected, all the records in his keeping for at least thirty years. And like his father, he wrote only for later peoples. After all, who else was there? True, all Book of Mormon prophet-writers knew, or sensed, that they were writing for latter-day peoples, that their record was to be buried and come forth "out of the dust" when the Lord saw fit. But those who preceded Mormon and Moroni also wrote for the instruction of succeeding generations of their own people. Not so with Moroni or his father. There were no succeeding generations of Nephites. Like his father, Moroni wrote for us—Jew, Gentile, and Lamanite alike. It is imperative that we read what these men say of their own lives and their concerns for us, that we absorb what they write, that we know their words are by no means fiction.

And so I turn to the books named after Mormon and Moroni, and yes, Ether—the final three books of the Book of Mormon. And I add 4 Nephi, too, that one-chapter book in which Mormon (clearly pressed for time) condensed three hundred years into forty-nine verses. But those verses teach the same lessons as the entire Book of Mormon. The same lessons Mormon and Moroni would teach with almost desperate intensity in their last writings, and that the first Nephi taught with great earnestness in the last chapters of his second book. The same lessons they urge us to learn, else why this record made for us? They bear testimony of Jesus Christ, and they insist that the record is true, that if we fail to accept it—and Christ as our Redeemer—we do so at our peril. We will be doomed to follow the path of their people, the path to spiritual darkness, moral degeneration, and bloody slaughter. Furthermore, they vow to meet us at the judgment bar of God, where we will be held accountable for our acceptance or non-acceptance of the record for which they paid an enormous price.

It should come as no surprise that modern-day prophets constantly teach precepts from the Book of Mormon and counsel us in no uncertain terms to read and study this sacred book. It carries the fulness of the restored gospel of our Lord and Savior, Jesus Christ. It will lead us to him. It is more important than a thousand gadgets and gizmos, than a thousand things we look to for entertainment and stimulation. It is more important than any theory, idea, sports team, or material thing on earth. With Moroni, I plead with you to make it yours. What you learn from it, and become because of it, is what you can take with you. Not a single iPhone or computer or ATV will go with you to paradise. What is in your head and your heart will go with you. Think about it. This book cannot be dismissed. It is a reality to be reckoned with.

II

MORMON'S SERMON AND LETTERS

Of singular importance are Mormon's sermon and the two personal letters I mentioned above, inserted into the record by Moroni. Mormon delivered the sermon while the church was still an organized body. We don't know the date of the sermon, but we know that Moroni deemed it so significant that he engraved it into his own record along with the letters. Mormon, a strong yet modest man, included none of his own sermons or letters in his record. Given the difficulty of hand-crafting metal plates and engraving tools in a devastated land, we have to ask ourselves why Moroni would select this sermon from presumably several, or even many, that must have been recorded during Mormon's ministry. Why preserve this particular message? Why preserve these particular letters? The only reasonable answer to such questions is that Moroni was moved or inspired to do so because of the inestimable significance of the sermon and the letters for latter-day peoples. For us.

Mormon's sermon, the earliest of the three precious documents, is recorded in Moroni 7. There, Moroni announces his father's subject as "faith, hope, and charity" (Moroni 7:1), but Mormon speaks of other things first. He speaks of gifts, beginning with "the gift of his [the Lord's] calling unto me" (7:2). Next he speaks of the gifts mortals give and the gifts they receive, stressing that everything that invites us to do good and to believe in Christ is a gift that comes from God. Mormon emphasizes the need for us to discern through the light of Christ, itself a gift, which gifts are from God and which are counterfeits from Satan.

Mormon then moves to the subject of faith, which is the key to "laying hold" of the good gifts that come from Christ (see 7:25). And

12

some of those gifts are manifest through miracles and the ministering of angels. I wonder if Moroni, at the time he inscribed his father's words, had any inkling of his future role in the restoration of the gospel of Jesus Christ in the nineteenth century. Did he know that he would be the angel assigned to deliver the record, the very record now in his protective care, to the people for whom he and his predecessors wrote? In effect, he would give us the gift twice, once in mortality and again in immortality.

It appears to me, as Mormon turns to the subject of hope, that he is using the doctrines of faith and hope in Christ, inseparable principles, to introduce the climactic point of his sermon. No one, he says, can have true faith and hope, and be "acceptable before God, save the meek and lowly of heart." But Mormon does not stop there. He goes one giant step farther, linking humility irrevocably to charity:

> If a man be meek and lowly in heart, and confesses by the power of the Holy Ghost that Jesus is the Christ, *he must needs have charity; for if he have not charity he is nothing; wherefore he must needs have charity.* (Moroni 7:44, emphasis added)

We have seen such a statement before in a place where the mortal Mormon and Moroni could not possibly have seen it: Paul's first letter to the Corinthians. I return to it here. Paul, like Mormon, whom he preceded by more than three hundred years, had been speaking of divine gifts prior to, and after, speaking of charity (see 1 Corinthians 12, and also 14). Paul elaborates on a statement similar to Mormon's after these introductory words at the conclusion of 1 Corinthians 12: "But covet earnestly the best gifts: and yet shew I unto you a more excellent way" (12:31). And what is that more excellent way? The ultimate gift. The way of charity, the way of Christ, and the gift of Christ himself. Hear Paul:

> Though I speak with the tongues of men and of angels, and have not charity, I am become as sounding brass, or a tinkling cymbal.
>
> And though I have the gift of prophecy, and understand all mysteries, and all knowledge; and though I have all faith, so that I could remove mountains, and have not charity, I am nothing.
>
> And though I bestow all my goods to feed the poor, and though I give my body to be burned, and have not charity, it profiteth me nothing. (1 Corinthians 13:1–3)

Already, we see an expansion of our customary application of the term "charity." Reread verse 3. *One can give all one's goods in assisting the poor and still lack charity.* So then, what is charity? It obviously has less to do with an act or gift *per se*, than with the spirit with which one acts or exercises understanding of prophetic gifts. Paul suggests that charity may be the most important mortal achievement, and yet it does not come by customary efforts at achievement, but by the reverse of such efforts. Nearly every definition of charity that Paul puts forth, and that Mormon later iterates, is the farthest thing possible from worldly acclaim or achievement—is in fact its antithesis, what Jesus and Mormon describe as meekness and lowliness of heart. A broken heart and a contrite spirit. Humility. The very opposite of pride.

The charity Paul and Mormon plead for is the cure for the ruinous spiritual cancer that toppled two ancient civilizations in the Americas and is now threatening a third: ours. *Charity, I have come to understand, is a shift in focus, and even priorities, from ourselves to others.* It is less an act or series of acts than a becoming—a becoming that prompts generous, loving acts. To be genuine, charity must work from the inside out.

One can scarcely read the lists of Paul and Mormon, lists that describe the person of charity in terms we too often forget, without perceiving that both men were obviously taught these things by the Spirit. Return with me now to Mormon as he concludes his sermon to those diminishing numbers of Nephites who still maintained a semblance of faith and hope or were at least still attending worship services. Let's pick up where we left off, with Mormon's words in Moroni's record, chapter 7, verse 45:

> And charity suffereth long, and is kind, and envieth not, and is not puffed up, seeketh not her own, is not easily provoked, thinketh no evil, and rejoiceth not in iniquity but rejoiceth in the truth, beareth all things, believeth all things, hopeth all things, endureth all things.

Paul's list of the qualities that define charity adds two more to Mormon's list: "vaunteth not itself," and "doth not behave itself unseemly." Repeat each of these qualities of charity aloud, slowly. Most of them describe humility; most are expressions of meekness and lowliness of heart; most are antidotes to pride.

Mormon then says it again: "If ye have not charity, ye are nothing," adding, as does Paul, that "charity never faileth" (Moroni 7:46; 1 Corinthians 13:8). Forgive the repetition as I cite verse 13 of 1 Corinthians 13:

And now abideth faith, hope, charity, these three; but the greatest of these is charity.

Faith, hope, and charity—this is the principal subject of the one sermon given by his father that Moroni chooses to inscribe in the record for latter-day peoples. Mormon further enjoins mortals to "cleave unto charity, which is the greatest of all," adding, like Paul, that "all [other] things must fail" (Moroni 7:46). Paul, as we saw above, even names other gifts that "shall fail," including such powerful gifts as "prophecies," "tongues," and "knowledge" (1 Corinthians 13:8). Think about it. The only gift guaranteed never to fail, so long as it is exercised, is charity. As I said before, charity does not fail; we fail of charity.

It is in verses 47 and 48 that Mormon takes us beyond the understanding that Paul only implies. We need to engrave this concept in our hearts. Charity, as the embodiment of the attributes both Paul and Mormon name, is defined by Mormon, once and for all, as "the pure love of Christ," the quality that encompasses every expression of forbearance, forgiveness, goodness, and humility—the power that "endureth forever" when all else fails. The love inherent in and exemplified by and through Christ is absolutely indestructible, incapable of failure. He will never cease to love, no matter what. And that is what we are asked to do—never cease to love as Christ loves, no matter what. Nephi knew this too. He saw our day and knew that many of us would be "lifted up in the pride of our eyes" (2 Nephi 26:20). He said, "The Lord God hath given a commandment that all men should have charity, *which charity is love. And except they should have charity they were nothing*" (26:30, emphasis added). This from Nephi, again approximately six hundred years before Paul wrote his first letter to the Corinthians.

And now, study with me the final verse of Mormon's sermon, a rich, stunning conclusion to a sermon in which Mormon is clearly endowed with grace and wisdom from on high. Whether Moroni was present in the congregation the day this sermon was delivered, we do not know. What we do know is that Moroni intended it to be etched into our hearts and minds. Here it is:

> Wherefore, my beloved brethren, pray unto the Father with all the energy of heart, that ye may be filled with this love, which he hath bestowed upon all who are true followers of his Son, Jesus Christ; that ye may become the sons of God; that when he shall appear we shall be like him, for we shall see him as he is; that we may

15

have this hope; that we may be purified even as he is pure. Amen.
(Moroni 7:48)

Clearly, charity is a gift for which we must pray "with all energy of heart." It is a gift "bestowed upon all who are true followers of Christ." As Carol Beus, an avid student of the Book of Mormon, has suggested to me, charity is not something we can give ourselves, but rather a gift "bestowed" upon us if we prepare ourselves to receive it. And how do we so prepare? I think we try earnestly to become like him, to strive consciously, daily, to be "meek and lowly of heart." We are not "puffed up" with self-importance. We unfailingly treat others with kindness, patience, and long-suffering. We forgive rather than blame; we neither think nor speak ill of others. We seek not our own exclusive satisfaction; we are not easily provoked; we bear whatever load falls to us; we endure. And as true followers and disciples of Jesus Christ, we believe unfailingly in him and his Atonement.

This is the way to become "the sons of God," spiritually reborn as children of Christ, "like him" in every possible way, bearing his spiritual genes just as a mortal child bears the biological genes of his mortal parents. The key is to be worthy of, and to receive, the gift of charity, the capacity for pure love. It is to be full of the pure love of Christ and void of any action, thought, or feeling that would be contrary to this purest of loves, contrary to any thought or feeling that he would have. As Mormon tells his people, and us, this must be our goal, our prayer, our great "hope"—to become like Christ our Savior. To "be purified even as he is pure." Imagine the possibility. Perhaps this is why "the greatest of these" is charity, because it is not only the way to him, it is also the way to purity and perfection through him. It is the way to become more like the very Son of God, even in this life.

This may seem unreachable to us, but Mormon appears to suggest otherwise in the first epistle of the two that Moroni inscribes into his record (Moroni 8). Mormon begins his letter by greeting "my beloved son, Moroni," and rejoicing that Christ has "called" Moroni "to his ministry" (8:2). Mormon tells his dear son that he prays for him "continually . . . unto God the Father in the name of his Holy Child, Jesus" (8:3). Mormon's main purpose in writing this letter is to correct the unacceptable practice of infant baptism that had apparently crept into the church in Moroni's part of the country. We are not told where

Moroni was at the time, but we do know that things were deteriorating and that the end of the Nephite nation was imminent. Mormon urges Moroni to "pray for" the people "in this part of the land" where in their pride they were "seeking to put down all power and authority which cometh from God; and . . . denying the Holy Ghost" (8:27–28).

But prior to these closing verses—even as Mormon denounces the perverse practice of baptizing "little children" who, the Lord has told him, "are whole" and "not capable of committing sin" (8:8), who are "alive in Christ, even from the foundation of the world" (8:12)—he speaks of "faith, hope, [and] charity." All three, Mormon insists, are lacking in anyone "that supposeth that little children need baptism" (8:14). Mormon says that he "speak[s] with boldness, having authority from God," and having no fear of man because "perfect love casteth out all fear" (8:16). He then declares that "perfect love," at least in some things, is possible for mortals. Hear his words:

> And I am filled with charity, which is everlasting love; wherefore, all children are alike unto me; wherefore, I love little children with a perfect love. . . . (8:17)

If Mormon can love "with a perfect love," with perfect charity, then perhaps it is possible for you and me to do likewise. The more I think about it, the more it seems to me that perhaps in this one thing—charity in its full range of meanings—we mortals can at least approach perfection in this life. We know that the perfection of godhood is the ultimate goal and that we are dependent upon the Atonement of Christ to bring us to a state of complete godly perfection in the eternities. Yet if we take Mormon at his word, mortal men and women are capable of loving "with a perfect love." I repeat: in this one thing, just maybe, if we develop and exercise the kind of love Mormon describes, we can become godlike. What hope that arouses in me just to contemplate the possibility! And a new determination to try.[1]

Mormon returns to the subject of charity—perfect love—later in his letter, presenting the doctrine in a series of causes and effects. First,

---

1. I note, however, that Paul seems to suggest that mortals can work only for and toward perfection, that the only absolute perfection is in Christ and the Father. Paul says, "For we know in part, and we prophesy in part. But when that which is perfect is come, then that which is in part shall be done away" (13:9–10).

he speaks of the baptism that comes through repentance and *faith*, the baptism that then brings a "remission of sins," which remission in turn "bringeth meekness, and lowliness of heart" (8:25–26). The latter are characteristics that both Mormon and Paul associate with charity. Mormon then enlarges on the subject of charity yet again, with additional layers of cause and effect. He states that "because of meekness and lowliness of heart cometh the visitation of the Holy Ghost" (layer one), "which Comforter filleth with *hope* and *perfect love*" (layer two), "which *love* endureth by diligence unto prayer" (layer three), "until the end shall come, when all the saints shall dwell with God" (8:26, emphases added). Here we have the three—faith, hope, and charity, with charity again in the climactic final position.

As though to underscore his point about the seminal role of meekness and lowliness of heart, Mormon adds, "Behold, the pride of this nation, or the people of the Nephites, hath proven their destruction except they should repent" (8:27). Again we must consider why Moroni includes this letter in his record. In my heart I know that he includes it because he is warning us, in this day, against the practice of infant baptism and more.[2] He is also warning us against pride. If we fail in humility, if we fail in charity, we are doomed to the same fate that befell both the Nephites and the Jaredites.

Briefly, now, turn with me to Moroni 9, the second letter from Mormon that Moroni inserted in the record. This letter was quite obviously written somewhat later than the previous one, perhaps considerably later. The situation that Mormon describes is heartbreaking. War has escalated to indescribable levels, and both Nephites and Lamanites have virtually lost their humanity. They are engaged in a blood bath that can only mean the end of the Nephite nation. Perhaps worse still, both sides have engaged in moral atrocities the likes of which Mormon can scarcely portray. The Lamanites "feed" their women prisoners "upon the flesh of their husbands, and the children upon the flesh of their fathers." But these barbarous acts, he says, do "not exceed [those] of our

---

2. The point Mormon is making here as he condemns the practice of infant baptism—"having authority from God to do so" (see Moroni 8:7–8, 16)—is that little children, and others who do not have the law, cannot be held accountable to it by a just God. They "cannot repent" for breaking commandments they have never heard, read, or understood (see Moroni 8 in general, and vv. 19 and 22–24 in particular).

people in Moriantum." There the Nephites rape, torture, and murder young Lamanite women and then "devour their flesh like unto wild beasts, because of the hardness of their hearts . . ." (Moroni 9:8–10).

I include the last phrase, "hardness of their hearts," because Mormon uses the phrase and similar expressions more than once in his letter, and it appears countless times in his abridgement. He says that his people "harden their hearts against" the word of God and are full of anger toward each other and toward him (9:4; see also v. 3). "If they perish," he says, "it will be like unto the Jaredites, because of the wilfulness of their hearts" (9:23). "Wilfulness," like hardness of heart, is most certainly a form of pride, which is contrary to charity just as "anger" is contrary to love. Mormon's words call to mind the curative for hardness and willfulness of heart that he urged in his sermon and his earlier letter: the pure love of Christ. Charity. It is the greatest of human and divine attributes and gifts, the characteristic without which we are nothing.

We can hear the anguish in his voice as Mormon describes a nation who "only a few years" ago "were a civil and a delightsome people" (9:12). But now "they have *lost their love*, one towards another; and they thirst after blood and revenge continually" (9:5). "O the depravity of my people!" Mormon cries. "They are without order and *without mercy*"; they are "brutal," "without principle, and *past feeling*" (9:18–20, emphases added). That loss of love, that hardness of heart, destroyed an entire people and left their land in shambles. We today must learn that lesson or we are lost.

III

MORMON'S LAST WORDS: WARNINGS BORN OF LOVE

We have been looking at some of Mormon's discourses, mainly those inserted into the record by his beloved son Moroni. Let's stay with the writings of Mormon for the moment, going specifically to the later words he inscribed into the record himself, words intended for our day and no other. Although prominent in the pieces we have just been considering, the doctrine of charity, or pure love, is not the announced subject of these other writings; but it is clearly a concern that underlies nearly everything Mormon wrote as Lehite civilization plunged toward chaos.[1] From the book of Mosiah through 4 Nephi, Mormon frequently adds his own brief commentary as he summarizes events or quotes from discourses and prophecies of earlier record keepers. He weaves these observations into the text so skillfully that we sometimes forget he is there.

At times, as in 3 Nephi 28:17 to 3 Nephi 30, Mormon steps boldly into the record as himself, to clarify certain matters—such as the nature of the three Nephite apostles who would not taste of mortal death—and to admonish us about the record and the gathering of Israel. These chapters, along with 4 Nephi, which traces the centuries following the Savior's ministry, seem almost like an introduction to Mormon's own "book," and to the themes that dominate his last writings. In 3 Nephi 29 and 30, preceded by two pertinent verses from 3 Nephi 28, Mormon issues warnings to our day if we refuse to receive the words of Jesus and

---

1. Mormon's writings actually begin with a short transitional section between the small plates of Nephi and Mormon's own abridgement of the large plates, a section I will refer to later.

of his prophets. In fact, he says, "it would be better for them if they had not been born" (3 Nephi 28:35; see also v. 34).

Mormon minces no words in 3 Nephi 29 when he speaks of the coming forth of the Book of Mormon in the latter days, for that event will signal the beginning of the Lord's promised fulfillment of his covenant with Israel. He declares that any who "spurn at the doings of the Lord" will feel "the sword of his justice" (3 Nephi 29:4). "Wo unto him," Mormon says repeatedly of those who deny revelation, prophecy, spiritual gifts, healings, and "the power of the Holy Ghost" (see 29:4–7; see also vv. 8–9). Chapter 30, which contains only two verses, is even more pointedly directed at latter-day Gentiles. I quote it in its entirety, for it is a compact statement of both warning and promise. Mormon could hardly be more earnest or more plain.

> Hearken, O ye Gentiles, and hear the words of Jesus Christ, the Son of the living God, which he hath commanded me that I should speak concerning you, for behold he commandeth me that I should write, saying:
> Turn, all ye Gentiles, from your wicked ways; and repent of your evil doings, of your lyings and deceivings, and of your whoredoms, and of your secret abominations, and your idolatries, and of your murders, and your priestcrafts, and your envyings, and your strifes, and from all your wickedness and abominations, and come unto me, and be baptized in my name, that ye may receive a remission of your sins, and be filled with the Holy Ghost, that ye may be numbered with my people who are of the house of Israel.

In 4 Nephi the theme of charity, though never named, literally jumps off the page. Fourth Nephi is the most condensed section of Mormon's entire abridgement, and as such, it allows us to see, in just a few pages, the decline of love and the rise of pride over centuries. This sort of thing is easier to overlook when it appears in the midst of lengthy narratives of many lives and countless events, but in 4 Nephi we can't miss it. Scan it with me as Mormon traces the frightful plummet, from the beatific faith and harmony that followed the Savior's ministry in the New World to unbridled wickedness and division. How could this happen, we ask, and so quickly? In our incredulity, we might cast our minds back across the last two centuries in our own nation. What would a short, one-chapter history of the United States look like?

Even a one-chapter history of the last five decades? Would tranquility and righteousness be dominant themes? I have to ask again and again with Moroni: Can we learn from their mistakes?

Granted, we did not have the equivalent of the two hundred years of peace and love that followed the Savior's ministry among the Lehites to stabilize our faith. But as a country, if contemporary standards of entertainment, speech, and dress are any indication, we seem to have boarded the Lehite fast train downhill since my childhood. Remember that after the Savior taught and ministered among them, the once-warring nations became one people, "all converted unto the Lord, upon all the face of the land, both Nephites and Lamanites, and there were no contentions and disputations among them, and every man did deal justly one with another" (4 Nephi 1:2). Again, this lovely state lasted two hundred years.

More to the point, perhaps, Mormon tells us that in the wake of the Savior's appearances and teachings among the Lehite people, "they had all things common among them; therefore there were not rich and poor, bond and free, but they were all made free and partakers of the heavenly gift" (1:3). Great prosperity abounded, the people rebuilt their cities, and they "did walk after the commandments which they had received from their Lord and their God," not the least of which were commandments to love one another and to be meek and lowly of heart. They faithfully fasted and prayed and met often, "both to pray and to hear the word of the Lord" (1:12). Mormon says repeatedly that "there was no contention among all the people" or "in all the land." The reason? "Because of the love of God which did dwell in the hearts of the people" (1:13,15,18). The pure love of Christ. That is the secret. Furthermore,

> There were no envyings, nor strifes, nor tumults, nor whoredoms, nor lyings, nor murders, nor any manner of lasciviousness; and surely there could not be a happier people among all the people who had been created by the hand of God.
>
> There were no robbers, nor murderers, neither were there Lamanites, nor any manner of -ites; but they were in one, the children of Christ, and heirs to the kingdom of God.
>
> And how blessed were they! For the Lord did bless them in all their doings. . . . (1:16–18)

It seems, however, that the prosperity that follows conversion and faithfulness is almost invariably a mixed blessing for the Nephite nation. Time after time throughout their history it leads to pride, ambition, and war. Even these last blessed people are not immune to the pride virus. Despite the "golden age" that ensued with the personal ministering of Christ among them, succeeding generations began to slide into the old patterns of ambition, faithlessness, and pride. Too predictably, prosperity eventually fostered pride and division as the wealthy and privileged separated themselves from the true, humble believers. I can hear the regret in Mormon's words as he writes:

> And now, in this two hundred and first year there began to be among them those who were lifted up in pride, such as the wearing of costly apparel, and all manner of fine pearls, and of the fine things of the world,
>
> And from that time forth they did have their goods and their substance no more in common among them.
>
> And they began to be divided into classes; and they began to build up churches unto themselves to get gain, and began to deny the true church of Christ. (1:24–26)

Furthermore, churches sprang up that denied "the more parts of [Christ's] gospel," and another "denied the Christ; and they did persecute the true church of Christ, because of their humility and their belief in Christ . . ." (1:27, 29). It is characteristic of the proud that they despise the humble, wanting nothing to do with charity.

This once-blessed people now "harden their hearts" (1:31, 34), seeking to kill the three disciples appointed to remain on earth. They did "smite upon the people of Jesus," who, significantly, "did not smite" in return (1:34). And then, in AD 231, "there was a great division among the people," with the "true believers in Christ" opposed by those who "did wilfully rebel against the gospel of Christ" (1:35–38). Once again we have "Nephites" and "Lamanites," believers and non-believers. Sadly, the rebels are "taught to hate the children of God, even as the Lamanites were taught to hate the children of Nephi from the beginning" (1:39). Hatred fills hearts among people where hearts only recently were filled with love. Moreover, the Nephites become contaminated by pride and vanity (1:43). Like the Lamanites, they succumb to the lure of Gadianton oaths and secret combinations, and in fewer than three hundred years after the Savior's ministry, "there were none that were righteous save it were the disciples of Jesus" (1:46).

Thus in 49 verses, Mormon summarizes the almost unbelievable tumble of a nation—a nation once thriving in unity through faith, humility, and abiding love—into heresy, pride, and hatred. Fourth Nephi frighteningly contrasts the beauty and grace of lives lived in perfect charity with the ugliness and terror of lives in which charity has been cast aside and trampled on.

The next book in the Book of Mormon is the record Mormon made in his own name, completing a summary history of his people by briefly describing his own era and experiences. He is now not only the abridger of the large plates of Nephi, but he is also the official record keeper of his day, after the manner of those writers who had preceded him in chronicling Nephite history for more than nine hundred years. He tells us that in writing the abridged record he "did forbear to make a full account" of the "wickedness and abominations" of his people, though he had done so in the larger record (Mormon 2:18). We can assume that Moroni left his father's abridged writings of his own era unchanged, writings that comprise chapters 1–7 of the nine-chapter book bearing Mormon's name. Moroni does, however, add to his father's book what we have as Mormon 8 and 9. I will visit those chapters in my expanded discussion of Moroni's writings.

Mormon learned when he was only about ten years old that in fourteen years he was to assume responsibility for the sacred Nephite records, records Ammaron (the last keeper of the records before Mormon) had hidden in a hill to protect them in turbulent times. Clearly, Mormon was divinely chosen for the assignment. By the time he was fifteen, he had been "visited of the Lord, and tasted and knew of the goodness of Jesus" (Mormon 1:15). Twice in 1:17 he refers to the "hardness" of his people's hearts and the cursing of the land because of it. Pride (hardness of heart) once more characterizes the Nephite people. So completely have these uncharitable people sealed themselves off from the Savior that they forbid Mormon to preach to them.

Even as they reject his teachings, they appoint the young Mormon, still in his teens, as "head of an army" (Mormon 2:2), and horrendous battles ensue with heavy losses. At first, Mormon takes heart when he sees his people mourning and sorrowing, but then he realizes theirs is only "the sorrowing of the damned," that "they did not come unto Jesus with broken hearts and contrite spirits, but they did curse God, and wish to die" (2:13–14). They remain prideful and devoid of humility and love.

For a time, the Nephite armies rally and prevail, and a treaty is signed with the enemy. But Mormon's people are still unwilling to repent and listen to his pleas to return to the Lord. As he says, "they did harden their hearts" (Mormon 3:3). Successful yet again in battle, his people "began to boast in their own strength, and began to swear before the heavens that they would avenge themselves" for their slain comrades (3:9). Pride and vengeance have taken over, and at that point, in his dismay, Mormon refuses to command the Nephite armies. We should note, however, that in spite of the great wickedness of his people, Mormon says that not only had he "led them many times to battle," but he

> . . . had *loved* them, according to the *love of God* which was in me, with all my heart; and my soul had been poured out in prayer unto my God all the day long for them; nevertheless, it was without faith, because of the hardness of their hearts. (3:12, emphases added)

There is perhaps no stronger evidence of Mormon's love for his people than the fact that, in spite of their bloodthirsty pride and stubborn wickedness, he later "repent[s]" of his "oath" to "no more assist them" and resumes command of their armies. He knows the cause is hopeless, "for they repented not of their iniquities, but did struggle for their lives without calling upon that Being who created them" (Mormon 5:1–2). Hopeless cause or not, they are his people, and he determines to live or die with them, fighting side by side, sealing his mortal fate with theirs.

We remember the words of Jesus when he said, "Greater love hath no man than this, that a man lay down his life for his friends" (John 15:13). And this is precisely what both Jesus and his servant Mormon did. Mormon loves as Christ loves, unconditionally, and he never stops praying for people who in no earthly sense deserve such love. He teaches charity by example as well as precept, and no mere mortal was more qualified to teach it than he was.

In chapter 3 of his book, Mormon leaves his narrative momentarily and speaks directly to latter-day readers—Gentiles, those of the house of Israel (all twelve tribes), and remnant Lehite peoples. "I write unto you all," he says, "all the ends of the earth" (Mormon 3:17–20). Mormon loves his own spiritually lost people, and he loves us. He loves us enough to plead, "I would that I could persuade all ye ends of the earth to repent and prepare to stand before the judgment-seat of Christ" (3:22). He loves us enough to make great sacrifices that we might have the sacred record.

Mormon returns to his narrative in chapter 4, chronicling the boasting (Mormon 4:8) and the increasingly hardened hearts (4:11) of his people. I can feel his anguish as he describes what the Lord has told him is the greatest wickedness ever seen in the house of Israel (4:12). Realizing that his people are hopelessly defeated by the Lamanites, Mormon goes "to the hill Shim" and "take[s] up all the records" (4:23). Then, in verse 8 of chapter 5, Mormon interrupts the narrative and addresses the reader directly. His concern is over how to write of the heart-rending last battles and atrocities without causing unbearable pain in his latter-day readers. His love for us is apparent as he says he does not want to "harrow up" our souls with a full account of the "awful scene of blood and carnage as was laid before mine eyes." Nevertheless, he knows that some knowledge of these things has to be disclosed. Therefore, he says,

> I write a small abridgement, daring not to give a full account of the things which I have seen, because of the commandment which I have received, and also that ye [the reader, you and I] might not have too great sorrow because of the wickedness of this people. (Mormon 5:9)

Mormon knows that latter-day Gentiles, "who have care for the house of Israel" (5:10), and Lamanite remnant peoples, whose ancestral history is told in the record, "will sorrow for the destruction of this people; they will sorrow that this people had not repented that they might have been clasped in the arms of Jesus" (5:11).

It is so like Mormon to be concerned that he not grieve us excessively in the day when we read his record, his account of a once "delightsome people" who "had Christ for their shepherd" and "were led even by God the Father" (5:17). Mormon's earnest care for our eternal safety and salvation is nowhere more apparent than in the final verses of chapter 5. In heightened agony at the possibility that we might fail just as his people failed, he cries out to us. Hear the warning born of love as he pleads:

> O ye Gentiles, how can ye stand before the power of God, except ye shall repent and turn from your evil ways?
>
> Know ye not that ye are in the hands of God? Know ye not that he hath all power, and at his command the earth shall be rolled together as a scroll?[2]

---

2. I was once quite baffled by the "scroll" simile with reference to the end of mortal time and earth. Now, I realize that the figure is a very apt one, signifying the finishing of a book or narrative.

Therefore, repent ye, and humble yourselves before him, lest he
shall come out in justice against you. . . . (5:22–24)

Mormon urges humility as well as repentance, for what is repentance but an expression of the deepest kind of humility? Read his words
again and feel his love, his great charity. The more I read Mormon's
words, the more I realize how Christlike he was as a mortal and how
great a debt of gratitude I owe him. He was a man of incredible valor, a
man of infinite sympathy, a man of God.

If there was ever a chapter in any book to break one's heart, it is
Mormon chapter 6. It chronicles the gathering of all the Nephite people
to the land of Cumorah for a last battle with their foes, a battle to the
death. We can scarcely imagine the terror of these fallen people as they
"await to receive" the myriads of armed "Lamanites marching towards
them" (Mormon 6:7; see also v. 8). Tens of thousands are "hewn down"
until every Nephite is killed but twenty-four souls and a few deserters.
Mormon himself is wounded, but Moroni has miraculously survived
while all his people are slain. Imagine the scene laid before Mormon's
eyes as the next day he views the carnage "from the top of the hill
Cumorah" (6:11), the "flesh, and bones, and blood" of his people scattered "upon the face of the earth" (6:15).[3] We can hear the love and the
grief in his voice as he cries aloud:

---

3.   Most Book of Mormon scholars are convinced that there are two hill
     Cumorahs—this one in Mesoamerica, in the midst of Nephite lands, and
     today's Cumorah in New York state. Moroni makes it clear that the final
     battles were fought in the same general area occupied by Jaredites and
     Nephites alike. He notes that the exiled Jaredite Omer, and his family,
     pass "by the place where the Nephites were destroyed" (Ether 9:3). And
     in referring to the flight of Heth's people from a plague of poisonous
     serpents, Moroni says that they fled "towards the land southward, which
     was called by the Nephites Zarahemla" (Ether 9:31). Moroni was there at
     the last battles, and he had records to attest to other matters of location.
     It appears to me that, although there were sizeable Nephite migrations
     north, the main bodies of both the Jaredites and Nephites/Lamanites
     spread out from, but essentially remained in one large central area—
     Mesoamerica. (I note, too, that there are no mentions of snowstorms and
     severe cold weather in the record, and New York state is hardly a tropical
     zone.) As for the records ending up in New York state, I'm quite sure that
     a God who can create worlds would have no trouble transporting a cache
     of records from one location to another.

O ye fair ones, how could ye have departed from the ways of the Lord! O ye fair ones, how could ye have rejected that Jesus, who stood with open arms to receive you!

Behold, if ye had not done this, ye would not have fallen. But behold, ye are fallen, and I mourn your loss.

O ye fair sons and daughters, ye fathers and mothers, ye husbands and wives, ye fair ones, how is it that ye could have fallen!

But behold, ye are gone, and my sorrows cannot bring your return . . .

O that ye had repented before this great destruction had come upon you. But behold, ye are gone. . . . (6:17–20, 22)[4]

These are not just numbers to Mormon, though the numbers are staggering. Among the dead are people from his village or city—wife, siblings, cousins, and perhaps children and grandchildren, "fathers and mothers," "husbands and wives." Ask yourself why Mormon would include his somewhat formal, though emotional, lament in the record, why he would share this great personal grief with us. I doubt his intent was to impress us with his poetic ability. But there is something about honest poetic expression that reaches us at the gut level. In this lament we feel not only Mormon's agony over his well-loved and lost people, but the intensity of his concern for us. In baring his soul, he is warning us again not to follow the course his people took, the course to destruction. I think it was love for us and the prompting of the Spirit that led Mormon to engrave these touching, personal verses in metal.

Amazingly, Mormon's last words in his own book (Mormon 7), and his final words as he prepares to hand the record to his son Moroni (see The Words of Mormon), demonstrate his unfailing love and concern for the descendants of the enemies and brutal annihilators of his people. This is a man who again demonstrates that he lived by the Savior's rules, including the injunction to love unfailingly, even one's enemies. Maybe especially one's enemies. In Mormon 7 he speaks directly to "the remnant of this people who are spared" (Mormon 7:1), the Lamanites. One would think that after what Mormon has experienced, he would hate the Lamanite survivors and all their offspring for generations to come.

---

4. For a poetic and musical treatment of this and surrounding passages, see "Mormon's Lament" in Arnold, Ozment, and Farr, *Sacred Hymns of the Book of Mormon*, 106-107.

But there are things he wants them to know, so that they will be spared the fate of his people and of their own ancestors. Hate is beneath this man. Love now seems to motivate his every thought and action.

First, he tells latter-day Lamanites that they are of the house of Israel, and he urges them to "lay down your weapons of war," permanently. Learn of your fathers, he says, "repent of all your sins and iniquities, and believe in Jesus Christ, that he is the Son of God," that he died and rose again from the grave. Through Christ, the dead are resurrected and the repentant redeemed to eternal happiness (7:2–7). Mormon writes that these remnant children of his enemies will read his words, and also the words of the record kept by the Jews (the Bible), and believe in Christ and know what marvelous works he wrought among their fathers. He promises them that if they will come to Christ and be baptized, by water and by the Holy Ghost, "it shall be well with you in the day of judgment." He concludes his book with a poignant "Amen" (7:10).

This attitude of pure love is reinforced in The Words of Mormon, a short interlude which was likely written within a few days of Mormon 7, just before Mormon himself was killed. The timing here is a little confusing because The Words of Mormon, comprising just eighteen verses, appears at the end of the small plates of Nephi, after the book of Omni and before the book of Mosiah, the first book abridged from the large plates. Nonetheless both The Words of Mormon and Mormon 7 were written in about AD 385. Mormon supposes that his son Moroni "will witness the entire destruction of my people"; and he prays that Moroni will survive to "write somewhat concerning them, and somewhat concerning Christ, that perhaps some day it may profit them" (Words of Mormon 1:2). Mark that purpose, stated unequivocally: the writing is not for peoples of his day, but for peoples "some day," today.

In this brief chapter Mormon explains that he has found the small plates of Nephi and added them to his abridgement, not only because they contain "prophecies of the coming of Christ" (1:4) but also because he has been directed to do so by the Spirit, in fulfillment of "a wise purpose" unknown to him at the time (1:6).[5] Even as he explains these and

---

5. Mormon couldn't have known, of himself, that a large section of the translated record (presumably the writings of Lehi) would be lost when Martin Harris borrowed it. But the Lord knew and prompted Mormon to attach the small plates to his abridgement so that we would have a record of the years chronicled on the lost manuscript.

other things, Mormon interjects yet another reference to the enemies who have destroyed his people. But again, he expresses no hatred or desire for vengeance. What he does express is the realization that the entire record, written over many centuries, is intended in large part for their posterity. What he expresses is love:

> And my prayer to God is concerning my brethren [the Lamanite remnant people], that they may once again come to the knowledge of God, yea, the redemption of Christ; that they may once again be a delightsome people. (1:8)

And so the formal writings of Mormon end, though as inspired commentator on the Nephite record he abridges, this great prophet is someone we encounter throughout the book.[6] He is a presence, a man of impeccable integrity, diligence, faith, and—as we have just seen—love.

---

6.   See in particular the discussion of Helaman 12 in Part Two, section VIII of this volume.

IV

MORONI: A LOVING APPEAL

I turn now to Moroni, a man whose writings clutch my heart and fire my mind as few other mortals' do. A special appeal emanates through his words that, I am sure, originated in his circumstances and his singular desire to awaken us to our danger and bring us to our Lord and Master, Jesus Christ. I am overwhelmed by his concern, his love for us, which would touch me more deeply and personally than even his father's love, if that were possible. We of this day and time are his audience, his only audience, and our reception of the record from his hands is his major concern—perhaps his sole concern other than the safety of the record—once his writing assignments are fulfilled.

It seems clear to me that Moroni had fully expected to conclude his personal writings with the two chapters he added to his father's book, Mormon 8 and 9. These chapters constitute a passionate farewell if there ever was one, a farewell warning and testimony of a man speaking to distant generations with all the fervor of his being and the angst of his circumstances. He writes of the disaster he has witnessed and the terrible loneliness he feels. He also writes, as we would expect, of the finished record, of the mortal who will bring it to light in the latter days, and of the prayers sent to heaven in that mortal's behalf by those who faithfully kept the record over the centuries.[1] Moroni sees our day all

---

1. The name of this latter-day prophet was known among the Nephites from the days of Lehi. In his patriarchal blessing to his son Joseph, Lehi quotes from the record of Joseph of Egypt (which was on the brass plates brought out of Jerusalem but has not survived into our Bible). The ancient Joseph says of the latter-day prophet that "his name shall be called after me; and it shall be after the name of his father" (2 Nephi 3:15).

too clearly, and it concerns him greatly. The power of his message is the power of truth and the power of the pure love of Christ.

When we ponder the despair that Moroni, a lone man, must have felt as he contemplated his destroyed world, we wonder how he could even go on, much less forge additional metal plates and inscribe them. His father instructed him to write, to finish the record, but how could he? How could he write of his people, especially when he feels totally inadequate (see Ether 12) as a writer? How could he garner the will to abridge the disheartening record of the Jaredite fall and add writings of his own, much less insert some of his father's writings into the record? Feel with me his desolation, his hopeless anguish, as he begins his lonely journey into a bleak, uncertain future:

> And my father also was killed . . . , and I even remain alone to write the sad tale of the destruction of my people. But behold, they are gone, and I fulfil the commandment of my father. And whether they will slay me, I know not.
>
> Therefore I will write and hide up the records in the earth; and whither I go, it mattereth not.
>
> Behold, my father hath made this record, and he hath written the intent thereof. And behold, I would write it also if I had room upon the plates, but I have not; and ore I have none, for I am alone. My father hath been slain in battle, and all my kinsfolk, and I have not friends nor whither to go; and how long the Lord will suffer that I may live I know not.
>
> . . . And behold also, the Lamanites are at war one with another; and the whole face of this land is one continual round of murder and bloodshed. . . . (Mormon 8:3–5, 8)

The plates are full, Moroni has no ore or tools with which to make new ones, and he is in the depths of sorrow. But somehow, he is lifted; somehow he finds the wherewithal to make additional plates. With what space he has left after completing the Ether abridgement and commentary, and with whatever crude engraving instrument he can manage to fashion, he creates a book that bears his name. And he adds to that book the sermon and two letters of his father Mormon that were discussed earlier. As I suggested then, given his situation, Moroni must have selected from the writings of his father with great care and with inspiration. How can we treat any of these precious discourses lightly? Indeed, anyone who takes the time to study the writings of Moroni knows that there is more to this man's legacy than one or two often quoted passages, important as those passages are.

We mortals are always interested in a dying person's last words. They hold a special fascination for those who have unknown miles yet to travel. All the more reason, therefore, that we should heed the words of the sole survivor of a once-thriving nation, a man who knew he could be killed at any moment by savage enemies feeding on hate. And what do we find Moroni writing about? Well, not about survival skills, or hatred for his enemies, or how he spent those lonely years (what a story that would be!), but about Jesus Christ, and the truth of the record, and *charity*. He also warns any who would presume to condemn the record.

Moroni's greatest hope is that we will learn from the mistakes of the Nephite and Jaredite people, that we will not follow the path they took, a path that ended in their physical destruction and spiritual damnation. The words Moroni writes, and the record he protects, are intended to set us, and keep us, on the path to everlasting life in the presence of God the Father and his Son Jesus Christ. The record is incontrovertible evidence of his love for those divine beings and for us—and of the love of those divine beings for him and for latter-day peoples.

It should come as no surprise, then, that in the aftermath of the last great war, Moroni takes up the themes of his father, Mormon, and the implicit themes that recur in Ether's record. Surely he also noted that those themes kept emerging among the experiences and writings of his other predecessors. Like many who wrote before him, Moroni addresses the matter of pride, and the lack of humility and meekness—the failures in charity—that were the undoing of his people. But as he begins his own additional record within his father's book, Moroni isn't talking about the pride of the Nephites. Having expressed his grief and borne witness of the record, he turns full attention to the abominable pride that he sees consuming latter-day peoples. He condemns "the pride of their hearts" that will lead them to deny "the power of God" and to defile their churches. He sees pride afflicting even some uninspired church "leaders" and "teachers," causing them to "envy" lay members (Mormon 8:28).

Moroni sees our day clearly and describes it with accuracy and energy. His concern for us is evident in verse after verse, for he is frighteningly blunt. He cares enough to sound a warning that we cannot afford to ignore. This is not guesswork or wild speculation on his part.

Oh no. The Lord has shown him the "day when these things [the writings in his care] shall come forth among you" (8:34). Moroni sees us becoming lax in obedience to the commandments and prideful in the extreme, and he fears for our souls. He cries out,

> O ye wicked and perverse and stiffnecked people, why have ye built up churches unto yourselves to get gain? Why have ye transfigured the holy word of God, that ye might bring damnation upon your souls? Behold, look ye unto the revelations of God; for behold, the time cometh at that day when all these things must be fulfilled. (8:33)

Should you still wonder if you and I are Moroni's intended audience, read this passage aloud several times:

> Behold, I speak unto you as if ye were present, and yet ye are not. But behold, Jesus Christ hath shown you unto me, and I know your doing.
> And I know that ye do walk in the pride of your hearts. . . . (8:35–36)

Again and again, Moroni cries out against the pride that afflicts all but "a few" in our day. Most "lift themselves up in the pride of their hearts, unto the wearing of very fine apparel, unto envying, and strifes, and malice, and persecutions," even polluting their churches "because of the pride of [their] hearts" (8:36).

If any could doubt that his subject is charity, in both the traditional and expanded senses of the term, he makes himself clear. We love things and appearances more than people:

> For behold, ye do love money, and your substance, and your fine apparel, and the adorning of your churches, more than ye love the poor and the needy, the sick and the afflicted . . .
> Why do ye adorn yourselves with that which hath no life, and yet suffer the hungry, and the needy, and the sick and the afflicted to pass by you, and notice them not? (8:37, 39)

From this point, Moroni launches into a doctrinal sermon that is as profound as it is pointed. He preaches basic gospel doctrine, with the record as his pulpit and God as his source. And again, he makes it plain that we are his audience:

> Behold, I speak unto you as though I spake from the dead; for I know that ye shall have my words.

Condemn me not because of mine imperfection, neither my father, because of his imperfection, neither them who have written before him; but rather give thanks unto God that he hath made manifest unto you our imperfections, *that ye may learn to be more wise than we have been.* (Mormon 9:30–31, emphasis added)

In this passage, Moroni is not talking about imperfections we might hope to find in the record, thinking to discredit it, but about imperfections we might discover in the mortal record keepers, in Moroni himself and his father, and those who preceded them. In effect, he is pleading for our charity, and pleading with us to learn from the record and be grateful to, rather than critical of, those who sacrificed that we might have it. Although he uses strong words, his only desire is a loving one, that we follow Christ and reject the destructive siren call of pride and selfishness.

As I read and reread Moroni's words in Mormon 9, I am struck yet again by the urgency in his voice. This is a man who cares for us enough to entreat the unbeliever—and possibly the lukewarm believer—to "turn ye unto the Lord; cry mightily unto the Father in the name of Jesus, that perhaps ye may be found spotless, pure, fair, and white, having been cleansed by the blood of the Lamb, at that great and last day" (9:6). Then Moroni delivers a sermon within a sermon, outlining the whole gospel plan in just five verses, 11 through 14. In those verses he covers the Creation, the Fall of Adam, redemption from sin and resurrection from death through Jesus Christ, and judgment. And should anyone need assurance, "God has not ceased to be a God of miracles" (9:15).

Imagine yourself in Moroni's situation, and then ask if the matter of the eternal happiness—or misery—of nameless generations, unborn, unknown, and perhaps undeserving, would be your main concern. Would you love them enough to put your own griefs and danger aside, to make their welfare your priority, to warn and plead and teach as this man does? We are moved by a similar, yet infinitely easier and safer, impulse to search out dead ancestors and perform saving ordinances for them. We are looking back while Moroni is looking ahead. He knows that most of those who hear his voice speaking from the record must come to faith, and to the Savior and his restored gospel themselves. They are accountable. We are accountable. Moroni knows, and we need to know, that there might be no rescue for us if we have chosen a worldly path and dismissed the record, the most powerful testimony of Jesus Christ on earth.

I can hear the pleading in Moroni's voice as he importunes us to "doubt not, but be believing, . . . and come unto the Lord with all your heart, and work out your own salvation with fear and trembling before him." He further entreats us to "be wise in the days of your probation; strip yourselves of all uncleanness; . . . yield to no temptation, but . . . serve the true and living God." Over and over again Moroni begs us to "doubt not, but be believing," "come unto the Lord with all your heart," "serve the true and living God" (9:27–29). Do these sound like the words of a detached observer? Not to me, they don't. I can feel Moroni's presence, his heartfelt insistence. This is charity the likes of which we see only in prophets and the Savior himself.

With these admonitions, and a reminder that "the Lord knoweth the things which we have written," Moroni expresses a desire that the prayers of Nephite prophets for the restoration of their "brethren . . . to the knowledge of Christ . . . may be answered according to their faith" (9:34, 36–37). And then he signs off, with a final "Amen," perhaps anticipating the possibility that he would end his own personal writings here. His first sentence in the book of Ether appears to make an immediate transition from that "amen." Moroni begins his abridgement with the phrase "and now," a transitional phrase: "And now I, Moroni, proceed to give an account of those ancient inhabitants . . ." (Ether 1:1), the people we call "Jaredites."

V

MORONI: THE BOOK OF ETHER, POIGNANT LESSONS

Moroni's verbal transition to the Jaredite record may be nearly seamless, but the leap back in time more than two and a half millennia is mind-boggling. I wonder what went through his mind as he took up Mosiah's translation of Ether's record, an account of an ancient people who once inhabited Nephite lands. It tells a story that began in love and faith and promise but ended in total carnage. Moroni's people followed the same route taken by this early people, with the same disastrous result. And all this in a land of promise, a land set aside for the Lord's chosen people. Moroni must have wept to read it, and wept to write a condensation of it. No wonder he warns us; no wonder he pleads with us to hold to faith in Christ. No wonder he begs us to love one another. He feared for us today because he could see us entering the same path to prideful, hate-filled destruction that consumed two doubly blessed nations of God's people in the promised land.

Very early in his abridgment of the Jaredite record, Moroni issues both a promise and a warning regarding this special land. After repeating the Lord's words to the brother of Jared, bright words regarding the choice land he had set aside for his people (see Ether 1:42–43), Moroni tempers that hopeful news with the Lord's warnings to any who inhabit the land. The Lord swore "unto the brother of Jared, that whoso should possess this land of promise, from that time henceforth and forever, should serve him, the true and only God, or they should be swept off when the fulness of his wrath should come upon them" (Ether 2:8). Moroni says it again, citing "the decrees of God concerning this land" as unimpeachable authority: "It is a land of promise; and whatsoever nation shall possess it shall serve God, or they shall be swept off when the fulness of his wrath shall come upon them." Then Moroni adds an important clarification: "And the fulness of his wrath cometh upon them when they are ripened in iniquity" (2:9).

Over and over, Moroni repeats this warning—almost word for word in verse 10, and with its particular application to us today in verses 11 and 12. He could not be more clear or more adamant than when he says, "And this cometh unto you, O ye Gentiles, that ye may know the decrees of God—that ye may repent, and not continue in your iniquities until the fulness come . . ." (2:11). And then he reminds us what this land of ours is all about and the solemn responsibility that rests on those blessed to inhabit it:

> Behold, this is a choice land, and whatsoever nation shall possess it shall be free from bondage, and from captivity, and from all other nations under heaven, if they will but serve the God of the land, who is Jesus Christ. . . . (2:12)

That is a very big *if.* I repeat: Moroni later reminds us that he has seen our day and knows our *doing* (Mormon 8:35, emphasis added). He is not speculating here; he knows us, and he has seen what can happen when a blessed people turn from their Maker.

Moroni is so filled with concern for our day that he continues to issue warnings to us, interspersing them insistently with his commentary accompanying Ether's record. Ether 5 is a case in point. He talks about the record that will come forth in the latter days and the Lord's instructions to the recipient of the plates. But Moroni attaches the following to a sentence, almost as an afterthought: "—and all this shall stand as a testimony against the world at the last day." And then he declares, with forceful purpose: "And now, if I have no authority for these things, judge ye; for ye shall know that I have authority when ye shall see me, and we shall stand before God at the last day. Amen" (Ether 5:4, 6).

Again in Ether 8, Moroni injects warnings to us, fearing that we will follow in the destructive path of the Jaredite and Nephite peoples. In verse 22 he warns specifically against any nation's upholding "secret combinations, to get power and gain." Such will be the ruin of those people and bring the wrath of God upon them. Then he adds:

"Wherefore, O ye Gentiles, it is wisdom in God that these things should be shown unto you, that thereby ye may repent of your sins, and suffer not that these murderous combinations shall get above you." The purpose of these combinations, he says again, is "to get power and gain," and if we allow these things to get hold among us, we will be overthrown and destroyed (Ether 8:23). It stands to reason that a proliferation of power-hungry mortals ushers in the shriveling of the pure love of Christ among those mortals.

The effect in Moroni's highly condensed account of the Jaredite people is like that of Mormon's condensed account in 4 Nephi. Once Moroni moves past the first generation of Jaredites, there is little cushioning to soften the impact. The narrative virtually races as the godless acts of hate and ambition accumulate. Moreover, a chagrined Moroni repeatedly interjects commentary intended to instruct his readers. Happily, though, the earlier chapters focus on miraculous events and a harmonious voyage, and Moroni dwells on those things in some detail. The account of Christ appearing in person to the brother of Jared, from whom we derive the name "Jaredites," is absolutely lovely. (See pages 77–79 in Part Two of this volume for a discussion of that event.) In time, however, with the introduction of kings, the decline in righteousness begins. And with that decline, charity in all its forms gives way to its opposites—power-hungry ambition, envy, moral decay, evil secret combinations, spiritual torpor, murderous acts, war, filial enmity, and betrayal. Especially filial enmity and betrayal.

In fact, after the early chapters, the whole story that Ether tells, and that Moroni briefly retells, can be seen as an exemplum. It chronicles one instance after another of the absence of love in families and of ambition and pride taking over hearts stripped of charity. If anything, at least for some time, the wickedness among the Jaredites is worse than that among the Lehite peoples. Secret combinations begin earlier, and the lack of love among siblings and between parent and child—especially of child for parent—infects generation after generation. (This lack of filial love was a problem in Lehi's family, but with one or two exceptions it does not seriously infect succeeding generations of his descendants. Some Nephites, however, were not above killing a chief judge or two in their pursuit of power and influence.)

As I ponder the second half of the book of Ether and picture Moroni condensing the history of kings slain or forced into captivity by their sons, I reach new understanding about the effect such work would have on a person in his circumstances. It becomes even clearer to me why he would include two of his father's letters, complete, in his own record. These letters, from Mormon to Moroni, with their tender expressions of love, must have leaped out in stark contrast to the dearth of such love in some Jaredite families. Perhaps it was reading of son after Jaredite son conspiring against father after father that made Moroni realize, even more, just how blessed he was to have the godfearing, loving Mormon for his father and how much Moroni loved him in return. In those letters, in addition to addressing matters of ministerial and moral urgency, Mormon repeatedly uses the endearing phrases "my beloved son" and "my son," along with other expressions of appreciation for a faithful son.

This is not to say that every Jaredite prince coveted his father's throne. There were good sons as well as bad sons, and the good sons often went to war against their brothers to restore their captive fathers to their rightful positions. But all in all, the state of affairs is rather grim, with even a daughter plotting against both her grandfather and her father, and a father casting a son into prison to die. No wonder Moroni warns us against hardheartedness and ambition; no wonder he engraves his father's sermon on faith, hope, and charity on the plates. No wonder he himself takes up the same subjects in his own writings. "The greatest of all," his father had said, is "charity," which is "the pure love of Christ" (Moroni 7:46–47). No wonder both father and son stress the importance of meekness and lowliness of heart, which, as we have noted before, is the opposite of pride and a manifestation of charity.

Rather than rehearse every instance of the failure of love and the rise of every power-hungry secret combination in the book of Ether, I will focus on Moroni's observations, his words on the theme of charity, which are directed squarely at his latter-day readers. In chapters 4 and 5 of Ether, Moroni also inscribes the Lord's words on a similar theme to those same readers. The Lord does not use the specific word "charity" when, in Ether 4:13–15, he enjoins both Gentiles and the house of Israel to come to him and cast off "the veil of unbelief." But he uses terms suggesting the opposite of charity when he describes the state of the non-believer as an "awful state of wickedness, and hardness of heart, and blindness of mind." And he urges latter-day peoples to "call upon the Father in my name, with a broken heart and a contrite spirit" (Ether 4:15; see also vv. 13–14, 16–17). The Lord is condemning pride and extolling humility.

In Ether 6, Moroni returns to his narrative to describe the sea voyage and arrival in the New World of this group of ancient immigrants. It is a journey and a new beginning marked by harmony and love, although the journey could not have been easy. Picture these early travelers in tightly closed vessels, bouncing both above and below the ocean surface—driven by the wind for 344 days, mind you. Notwithstanding their physical circumstances, they "sing praises unto the Lord," and the brother of Jared "did thank and praise the Lord all the day long; and when the night came, they did not cease to praise the Lord" (Ether 6:9). In contrast, we remember a Lehite voyage fraught with dissension and hate that nearly tore Lehi's family apart. Moreover, when this early group, who must have been physically frazzled and weary, reached "the shores of the promised land they bowed themselves down upon the face of the land, and did humble themselves before the Lord, and did shed tears of joy before the Lord, because of the multitude of his tender mercies over them" (6:12). They kept the Lord in their humble, grateful hearts all the way, and he blessed them with the pure love of Christ.

Unfortunately, once the travelers settle and begin to multiply, they ask for a king. Within two generations, as told in Ether 7, the trouble begins, and one king is overthrown by one son and restored by another. From there, it is sons and grandsons against fathers and grandfathers, and against each other, in a tangle of ambition and enmity. For a time, the country is divided into two kingdoms. Moroni must have seen that division as a forerunner of the disjunction that would plague the Nephites throughout most of their stormy history.

In Ether 8 and 9, Moroni sketches one of the ugliest of all the Jaredite stories. The events of this sad tale describe a complete absence of charity, or any kind of familial caring and human goodness. A son, Jared (but unworthy of the name), lusts after power, "his heart [set] upon the kingdom and upon the glory of the world" (Ether 8:7). Jared buys into his own daughter's scheme to behead his father and take the throne. And his father's friend Akish is to do the beheading, no less, with the daughter as a prize. What Jared hadn't planned on, however, was that his father, Omer, would be warned by the Lord and able to make his escape to a remote area. Another thing Jared hadn't planned on was the ambitions his daughter entertained for herself, ambitions matching those of her new husband. Secret combinations are formed, after the order of Satan and Cain, and Jared is beheaded "as he sat upon his throne" (Ether 9:5), compliments of Akish and his bride.

Moroni includes some of the gruesome details in his account, and he interjects an impassioned warning to our day, especially to Gentiles, against secret combinations. Twice he tells us why they must be guarded against:

> And whatsoever nation shall uphold such secret combinations, *to get power and gain*, until they shall spread over the nation, behold, they shall be destroyed . . .
>
> Wherefore, O ye Gentiles, . . . suffer not that these murderous combinations shall get above you, which are built up *to get power and gain*—and the work, yea even the work of destruction come upon you . . . if ye shall suffer these things to be. (Ether 8:22–23, emphases added)

Moreover, these evil combinations seek "to overthrow the freedom of all lands, nations, and countries." They are instruments of the devil, "who hath hardened the hearts of men" (8:25). Moroni writes, he says, by commandment of the Lord, "that Satan may have no power upon the hearts of the children of men, but that they may be *persuaded to do good* continually" (8:26, emphasis added). Always, always, the impure hatred of Satan seeks to undermine and destroy the pure love of Christ. Satan's weapons against charity are ever pride, selfishness, envy, and the lust for power.

As Moroni continues his narrative, we learn that Akish, newly enthroned via the murder of his father-in-law, has no love for his own son. He is in fact, "jealous of his son," and sends him to prison to starve to death (Ether 9:7). But where Akish is "desirous for power," his people are "desirous for gain," and therefore subject to bribery. Unfortunately for Akish, it is his own sons who, having acquired their father's taste for power, are able to bribe "the more part of the people" to follow them in rebellion against their father. And the beat goes on until all-out warfare ensues. That war reduces the population to "thirty souls, and they who had fled with the house of Omer" (9:11–12). Pause on that statistic. The Jaredite nation is pared down to Omer's family and friends, and just thirty others. Discarding charity, or any semblance of concern for others, nearly wiped out the entire Jaredite civilization centuries before its final complete demise.

The lesson is learned, though only temporarily, and a few generations of righteousness and peace follow. Omer's son, Emer, "even saw the Son of Righteousness, and did rejoice and glory in his day; and he died in peace" (9:22). Two generations later, however, the "secret plans . . . of old" emerge once more, and Heth, desiring his father's throne, slays "him with his own sword" and "reign[s] in his stead" (9:26–27). The problem with rule by kings is vividly apparent in these accounts. Any dissident who wants the throne need only gather (or bribe) supporters and kill the reigning monarch to get it. The possibility of gaining power by a system of popular vote never occurs to these folks. It takes a great "dearth" (famine) and a plague of poisonous serpents to humble them. Once again humility is the key to survival and prosperity, but we mortals never seem to remember that for long.

Chapters 10 and 11 read like a broken record, with self-indulgence and the overthrow of kings softened by a period of amazing prosperity and happiness. Which doesn't last, of course. The Jaredite version of the Gadianton robbers appears again, and king after king is overthrown, sometimes in a rebellion of son against father, sometimes in a rebellion of brother against brother, sometimes neither. That old song comes to mind—"Where is the love?" Where, indeed. Finally, at the end of chapter 11, we have the birth of Ether, the last Jaredite prophet and historian.

For the moment, I am jumping over Ether 12 in order to continue a brief assessment of the narrative of Ether's people as they rampage toward oblivion. I will return to chapter 12 because it is solely Moroni's discourse and, in my mind at least, makes a splendid companion piece with the final chapter of his own book, Moroni 10—especially on the subject of charity. It is a subject that seems to have risen to the top of Moroni's consciousness as he wrote about the decay and destruction of the Jaredite nation.

Clearly, Moroni is impressed with Ether as a man and a prophet. Not only does he relate some of Ether's splendidly inspired prophecies, but he lengthens his account of the days of Ether—possibly because Ether himself is more detailed in writing what he himself observed. By the time Ether arrives on the scene, prophets were not "esteemed" among the Jaredite populace. In fact, they "cast him out; and he hid

43

himself in the cavity of a rock by day," from which cavity "he made the remainder of this record, viewing the destructions which came upon the people, by night" (Ether 13:13–14). Then, "in the second year," the Lord sends Ether to offer Coriantumr, the king, a chance to save himself and his subjects from destruction. If he and his household repent, he and his people will be spared. If they refuse, only Coriantumr will survive to be discovered by a later people who will "receiv[e] the land for their inheritance." They refuse, all right, and promptly seek "to kill Ether," but he manages to escape to his cave (13:20–22). Wars heat up as wickedness and anger engulf Ether's nation. "All the people upon the face of the land were shedding blood, and there was none to restrain them" (13:31).

Chapters 14 and 15 continue to document the madness of unrestrained killing of leaders and eventually everyone else. Secret combinations are rampant, the people are divided into two angry camps, and hate-filled hearts will not listen to reason or exercise restraint. Only Coriantumr, seeing that "nearly two millions of his people" have been "slain by the sword," begins to repent. He writes to Shiz, current head of the opposition, offering to "give up his kingdom for the sake of the lives of his people." Shiz replies that he will spare Coriantumr's people if Coriantumr will surrender to him "that he might slay him with his own sword." This challenge serves only to stir Coriantumr's people "to anger against the people of Shiz," who are in turn "stirred up to anger," and war ensues again (Ether 15:2–6).

So bereft are these people of any semblance of faith or hope or the pure love of Christ, that they spend four years gathering their forces for a final, to-the-death battle. They arm women and children as well as men and march to their doom. After two days of bloodshed, Coriantumr writes again to Shiz, repeating his previous offer. But it is too late.

> The Spirit of the Lord had ceased striving with them, and Satan had full power over the hearts of the people; for they were given up unto the hardness of their hearts, and the blindness of their minds that they might be destroyed; wherefore they went again to battle. (15:19)

Six more days they fight; five more nights they sleep on their swords, "drunken with anger" (15:22). By the last night, only thirty-two are left on one side and twenty-seven on the other. That night those fifty-nine "ate and slept, and prepared for death on the morrow" (15:26). Death is what they get, and finally only Shiz and Coriantumr are left. Moroni, perhaps hoping to shock us to our senses, includes in his account the gory details of the last encounter between the two men, an encounter that leaves Coriantumr barely alive and Shiz dead, his head smitten off by the sword of his foe.

This stunning and horrifying account illustrates the costs of unbridled hatred, the costs of lust for power and secret combinations, the costs of godlessness, and the costs of willful denial of the pure love of Christ.

VI

MORONI: CHARITY, ALWAYS AND FOREVER

In chapter 13 Moroni reports some of Ether's inspired prophecies and courageous acts, but our introduction to Ether comes in the opening verses of chapter 12, prior to the final battles of his people. Moroni has been working with Ether's record and now he pauses to allude directly to Ether's teachings. He allots only a few verses to Ether here, but they are enough to give us a glimpse of a dedicated, inspired prophet of God who "did prophesy great and marvelous things unto the people, which they did not believe, because they saw them not" (Ether 12:5). The three subjects in Ether's exhortations that Moroni emphasizes are faith, hope, and "good works." Surely, Moroni saw the link to his father's sermon and his own writings. It would seem, in fact, that the words of Ether trigger the "sermon" Moroni delivers to us in the thirty-five verses that follow.

Ether 12 becomes another of Moroni's extremely important discourses, of the same intensity as those in Mormon 8 and 9, Moroni 10, Ether 4 and 5, and a major segment in Ether 8. But Ether 12 is both long and powerful, and it appears that yet again Moroni had thought to conclude his own writings with this intervention in the Jaredite record. We sense that after summarizing Ether's teachings, Moroni felt compelled to reinforce what Ether had said about faith and hope and then add his own personal exhortations on charity. It was a subject he had visited before and would revisit, with fervor, at the end of his record and near the end of his life.

Moroni launches immediately into a formidable treatise on the necessity of faith in Christ, mentioning hope also, which derives from faith. He then cites many instances of the faith exercised by those who preceded him, naming great Nephite teachers like Alma, Amulek, Ammon, and the brothers Nephi and Lehi just decades before the birth of Jesus. In Ether 12:22 Moroni crosses into his broader purpose, using faith as his springboard:

> And it is by faith that my fathers have obtained the promise that these things [the written record] should come unto their brethren through the Gentiles; therefore the Lord hath commanded me, yea, even Jesus Christ.

Like his predecessors, Moroni speaks of the Lamanites, who were so often enemies of the Nephites, as "brethren." It is for them, and for the latter-day Gentiles who will take the record to them, that the record is made and preserved. No matter what, the faithful record keepers never ceased to love their enemies—and to pray and sacrifice for them.

What strikes me about the next group of verses, Ether 12:23–29, is the prominence of the theme of humility—charity in the sense that both Paul and Mormon speak of it. Moroni, painfully sensitive to what he fears is "weakness in writing" among the Nephite recorders, goes to the Lord for counsel. He worries that "the Gentiles will mock at these things, because of" that weakness. His concern is most certainly not for his own image, but for the reception of the record when it is brought forth. He says that the Lord has made the spoken words of the Nephite prophets "powerful and great, even that we cannot write them; wherefore, when we write we behold our weakness, and stumble because of the placing of our words," adding, "and I fear lest the Gentiles shall mock at our words" (Ether 12:23–25). I smile at this and wish I could assure Moroni that this "Gentile" reader, and many like me, find the written words in this remarkable record to be extremely "powerful and great." Still, Moroni's humility is a lesson to me.

The Lord assures his last Nephite prophet that he need not fear the arrogance of disbelievers: "Fools mock, but they shall mourn; and my grace is sufficient for the meek" (12:26). Furthermore, the Lord says, "If men come unto me I will show unto them their weakness that they may be humble; and my grace is sufficient for all men that humble themselves before me." Meekness, in fact, is strength and a gift ("I give unto men weakness that they may be humble"). The Lord vows that if mortals "humble themselves before me, and have faith in me, then will

I make weak things become strong unto them" (12:27). Then he adds a climactic promise:

> Behold, I will show unto the Gentiles their weakness, and I will show unto them that faith, hope, and charity bringeth unto me— the fountain of all righteousness. (12:28)

In the verses that follow, Moroni's response to the Lord indicates that he sees the significance of the three qualities, and he sees that they are inseparably linked. Mortals must adhere to all three in order to receive their eternal inheritance. Again, as always, charity is named last, as the pinnacle or capstone of human character and blessedness. Still speaking to the Lord, Moroni remembers the Lord's having said that he has "loved the world, even unto the laying down of [his] life for the world" (12:33). I think Moroni understands, perhaps more completely now, the full meaning of the phrase his father had used to define charity: "the pure love of Christ." He understands that mortals must love as Christ loves:

> And now I know that this love which thou hast had for the children of men is charity; wherefore, except men shall have charity they cannot inherit that place which thou hast prepared in the mansions of thy Father. (12:34)

If we read Moroni's next statement too quickly, we might miss something very important:

> Wherefore, I know by this thing which thou hast said, that if the Gentiles have not charity, because of our weakness, that thou wilt prove them, and take away their talent, yea even that which they have received, and give unto them who shall have more abundantly. (12:35)

I see here a seeming allusion to the parable of the talents (which Jesus might well have taught among the Nephites), with charity as the "talent," the gift which mortals may "have received." In the "proving" of them, if they have not exercised this "talent," this gift of charity, the Lord might well "take away their talent" and "give unto them who shall have more abundantly."[1] Moroni might well be saying that the pure

---

1. In the Lord's words to the first Nephi, which Nephi records in some of his final writings, the Lord seems to speak—in at least a glancing allusion— of wisdom in similar terms. Those who "hearken" to him "shall learn

love of Christ is a gift we could lose if we bury it by failing to exercise and enhance it. This passage opens a new door of thought for me. What if in teaching the parable of the talents in the New Testament, Jesus was indeed talking about charity, charity in its various forms and degrees, as the metaphorical talents given the servants? There might well have been a larger, unrecorded, context for the parable.

Continuing the theme, verse 36 speaks of charity as a gift through the grace of God, for Moroni prays to the Lord "that he would give unto the Gentiles grace, that they might have charity." Then the Lord teaches Moroni an important principle: "If they have not charity it mattereth not unto thee, thou hast been faithful" (12:37). Our concern is with the kinds of persons *we* are, with how we treat others, regardless of what others do to us. We are to extend love even if others mock or hate us. The Lord concludes by reiterating what he had said earlier: out of the humility that allows us to see our weaknesses comes strength (12:37).

At this point Moroni initiates the conclusion of this particular discourse and seemingly also of his personal message to latter-day readers. First, he "bid[s] farewell unto the Gentiles," *us*, and then "also unto my brethren whom I love" (12:38). Again, the "brethren" whom he loves are the descendants of the Lamanite enemies who defeated him and brutally maimed and killed all his people in the last great battles of the two nations. How many of us could love such brethren? Then he bears powerful testimony of Christ in a passage that emphasizes the fact that the Lord Jesus, the very Son of God, sets the example of charity and meekness by communicating, with great patience, and in person, with a mortal. Hear Moroni's witness after he speaks of a future meeting with you and me "before the judgment-seat of Christ" (12:38). These are not the words of a pretender:

> And then shall ye know that I have seen Jesus, and that he hath talked with me face to face, and that he told me in plain humility, even as a man telleth another in mine own language, concerning these things. (12:39)

wisdom; for unto him that receiveth I will give more; and from them that shall say, We have enough, from them shall be taken away even that which they have" (2 Nephi 28:30).

And so, after one more reference to his "weakness in writing" (12:40), Moroni ends his discourse with a prayer that bears witness of his sincere concern and love for us in this day. In words that echo his father's conclusion to his second letter (see Moroni 9:26), Moroni asks that "the grace of God the Father, and also the Lord Jesus Christ, and the Holy Ghost, which beareth record of them, may be and abide in you forever. Amen" (12:41). Here is a remarkable man who lives by what he teaches. There is no guile or hypocrisy in him. There is faith, hope, and the greatest of these, charity.

Although he may have thought to end the record with his father's letter, or to let his previous exhortations in the books of Mormon and Ether stand as his final words to latter-day readers, an aging Moroni adds a final book. And it is a memorable one. As I suggested earlier, perhaps no scripture in the entire Book of Mormon—with the possible exception of the first Nephi's "I will go and do the things which the Lord has commanded . . ." (1 Nephi 3:7)—is more familiar or is cited more often than is verse 4 of Moroni 10:

> And when ye shall receive these things, I would exhort you that ye would ask God, the Eternal Father, in the name of Christ, if these things are not true; and if ye shall ask with a sincere heart, with real intent, having faith in Christ, he will manifest the truth of it unto you by the power of the Holy Ghost.

When it comes to testing the authenticity of the Book of Mormon, a reader need not rely wholly on the word of believing mortals, or even the testimonies of ancient record keepers, valid and valuable as they are. A reader can go to the Source, with a capital "S". Don't believe me if you don't want to, Moroni says. Go to a higher authority—the highest authority—God himself. It is worth noting, however, that even though the test has broad application to any and every reader, Moroni directs his injunction especially to "my brethren, the Lamanites" (Moroni 10:1). Like his father, Mormon, he wants to ensure that later generations of his misguided enemies take this record into their hearts and lives, letting it direct them back to their Eternal Father and his Son. His concern for these blood enemies never falters; it is constant evidence of his unceasing charity. In this one discourse, Moroni uses the phrase "my brethren" or "my beloved brethren" four times (10:1, 8, 18, 19).

While still addressing his "brethren" in particular, Moroni speaks of a variety of spiritual gifts, in more specific terms than Mormon had done in his sermon, but his next subject is the same: faith, hope, and charity. He stresses that the three are interdependent and that all are necessary for salvation:

> Wherefore, there must be faith; and if there must be faith, there must also be hope; and if there must be hope there must also be charity.
>
> And except ye have charity, ye can in nowise be saved in the kingdom of God; neither can ye be saved in the kingdom of God if ye have not faith; neither can ye be saved if ye have no hope. (10:20–21)

Moroni teaches us that there is no such thing as true faith or real hope, in the absence of charity. Then he broadens his intended audience to encompass "all the ends of the earth," emphasizing the fact that any good works performed by mortals are done "by the power and gifts of God" (10:24).

I am sorely tempted to quote verses 27 to 34 in their entirety. Short of that, I lovingly "exhort" you to pick up the Book of Mormon and read the last page of it yourself. This much I must quote, however, because Moroni delivers a testimony to the truth of the record that rings with conviction. I challenge anyone to read this statement out loud, with a mind and heart open to truth, and then deny the authenticity of the Book of Mormon:

> The time speedily cometh that ye shall know that I lie not, for ye shall see me at the bar of God; and the Lord God will say unto you: Did I not declare my words unto you, which were written by this man, like as one crying from the dead, yea, even as one speaking out of the dust? . . .
>
> And God shall show unto you that that which I have written is true. (10:27, 29)

As Moroni prepares to close the record, once and for all, and then to hide it until a much later day, he urges his readers to "come unto Christ," to "deny yourselves of all ungodliness, and love God with all your might, mind and strength" (10:30, 32). I am reminded, in reading that powerful admonition to love God mightily, that the phrase "pure love of Christ" most surely has a dual application. The words "love of" can also mean "love *for*." Given that very real possibility, true charity must embrace mighty love for God as well as Godlike love for fellow mortals. In reality, as Jesus himself taught, the two are alike and go hand in hand. Again and again his words in response to one of the Pharisee's "trick" questions come to mind:

> Then one of [the Pharisees], which was a lawyer, asked him a question, tempting him, and saying,
>
> Master, which is the great commandment in the law?
>
> Jesus said unto him, Thou shalt love the Lord thy God with all thy heart, and with all thy soul, and with all thy mind.
>
> This is the first and great commandment.
>
> And the second is like unto it, Thou shalt love thy neighbour as thyself.
>
> On these two commandments hang all the law and the prophets. (Matthew 22:35–40)

One cannot truly love God and hate any of his children, nor can one love any of God's children, in the truest sense, and hate that person's Maker.

Jesus teaches this same principle in the Sermon on the Mount and again in his ministry among the Nephites after the great cataclysm has destroyed the more wicked among them:

> Ye have heard that it hath been said, Thou shalt love thy neighbour, and hate thine enemy.
>
> But I say unto you, Love your enemies, bless them that curse you, do good to them that hate you, and pray for them which despitefully use you, and persecute you. (Matthew 5:43–44; see also 3 Nephi 12:43–44)

Jesus expands on this teaching in verses 45–47 in the Matthew account, and then concludes with a seemingly curious, even irrelevant, statement in verse 48 of both accounts—again, with slight variations: "Be ye therefore perfect, even as [I or] your Father which is in heaven is perfect." Why, we ask, does Jesus give the commandment to be perfect at the end of an injunction to love all mortals, including our enemies? What have the two to do with each other? Maybe Jesus is saying, as his prophet Mormon would suggest centuries later, that in this one thing, in feeling and exercising pure love in mortality, it is possible to be perfect. Maybe Jesus is also saying that perfection is possible only for those whose love embraces all other mortals, even enemies.

Remembering this commandment from the Savior himself at least partly explains why both Mormon and Moroni never ever express hatred for their enemies, their "brethren," why they continue to love them and their own godless, fallen people. The words of the risen Christ have taken hold in their hearts.

Most assuredly, the doctrine of charity is paramount in the teachings of the last great Nephite leaders and record keepers. If we learn nothing else from them, we must learn that charity, in its multitude of forms, may well be the most important of all human attributes. The most important because it is the most Godlike. The most important because it stands against the destructive forces of pride, envy, greed, ambition, anger, selfishness, impatience, hate, and the list goes on. Wherever we see the pure love of Christ operating among mortals, pride, self-vaunting, anger, and all the rest are absent.

THE *Last Words* OF THE *First Prophets*

I

NEPHI'S WARNINGS AGAINST PRIDE

Remembering that everything in the Book of Mormon from the book of Mosiah through 4 Nephi is funneled through Mormon's mind, we might well expect books in the major portion of the Book of Mormon to reflect Mormon's deepest concerns. We should never doubt, however, that Mormon's selection or summary of revelations, narratives, sermons, events, and counsel from the writings and teachings of his predecessors was inspired by the Lord. By that same inspiration, he left untouched the engravings on the small plates of Nephi. They comprise 1 and 2 Nephi, Jacob, and the short books of Enos, Jarom, and Omni. Mormon had already abridged the whole of the large plates engraved by Nephi before he came across the set of smaller plates, also engraved by Nephi, containing those books.[1] The Lord knew, if Mormon didn't, why they had to be attached to his abridgement. The writings on the small plates were to be our only record of

---

1. See 1 Nephi 9 and 19; 2 Nephi 4:14-15; and 2 Nephi 5:30-33, where Nephi discusses these matters and describes his role in preparing the two sets of plates according to divine instructions.

Nephi and his people—at least for the foreseeable future.[2]

What Mormon would see in Nephi's writings on the small plates must have seemed a rehearsal for what would transpire throughout the record, from beginning to end, and among Mormon's contemporaries. And surely Mormon must have apprehended a theme by now only too familiar to him. Indeed, pride and lack of charity plagued Nephite society from the beginning. Over and over again, Mormon had read of the destructive cycle being repeated: a blessed people become prosperous, but in their prosperity, they grow proud and uncharitable. Pride leads to contention and dissent, which in turn lead to war and suffering. Only then do the hardhearted become humble and loving again. As we have seen, Mormon's own people were in the downward spiral of that cycle for much of his lifetime. In the end, however, there was no redeeming upswing. It should not surprise us, therefore, to see references to this weakness in the Nephite character throughout Mormon's abridgement, in the discourses he quotes from Nephite leaders, and in his own writings.

Given that Mormon was divinely led in selecting materials to include, we should pay particular attention to the addresses and discourses he left intact. I am grateful that he also included his personal commentaries and observations along the way. So many times we read at the conclusion of a particular narrative, "And thus we see . . ." This is Mormon, speaking directly to us. He is such a presence in the Book of Mormon that I almost know him as a wise personal friend, sent to guide me. We can't possibly miss the fact that, first and foremost, the discourses he quotes and the narratives he summarizes bear powerful testimony of Jesus Christ. They repeatedly allude, in elevated language, to the Savior's atoning sacrifice and the love he represents, both before and after his mortal birth and ministry. In addition to bearing testimony of Christ and teaching other specific doctrines, the discourses and narratives speak to the matter of human character. They show repeatedly the disastrous consequences of casting charity aside.

You and I know that we can never say enough about the first, about Christ and his ministry and atoning mission. Many have written

---

2. See Doctrine & Covenants 10:31ff where the Lord discusses this matter in his instructions to Joseph Smith regarding the lost manuscript pages and his reasons for not allowing a retranslation of those pages.

eloquently on that precious subject.[3] But I think many of us, myself included, have paid too little attention to the second, to the essential doctrine of charity, and what happens when we fail to be a charitable people.[4] Recalling Mormon's words on the matter and his perception of the role such a failure played in the destruction of the Nephite nation, we can only take these things as a warning to our own day against following such a course.

I can't help thinking, too, that as Mormon read Nephi's record on the small plates, he might have seen in the lives of Laman and Lemuel a microcosmic parallel of the whole of Nephite history. Like succeeding generations of Nephites, the two men swing up and down, up and down, rebelling and repenting, rebelling and repenting, as they cycle from pride and hatred into humility and amenity, and then back to pride and hatred. Their repentance, like their humility, is temporary, though they be brought to their knees by angels and other miraculous manifestations. Reading about their vacillation is like seeing Nephite history on the screen in fast forward mode.

We are not blessed to have a great many of Lehi's discourses in our record, though fortunately Nephi recorded some of his father's prophecies, visions, revelations, and counsel to his sons on the small plates. As Lehi nears the end of his life, he pleads with the often rebellious Laman and Lemuel to "awake," fearing for them because of "the hardness of [their] hearts" (2 Nephi 1:13, 14, 17) and enjoining them to "be determined in one mind, and in one heart, united in all things" (1:21)—to be loving men rather than contentious men.

---

3.   I make special mention here of a remarkable book by Elder Jeffrey R. Holland, a book that focuses on Christ as he is prophesied and taught, and as he teaches, among Book of Mormon peoples. Its title, *Christ and the New Covenant: The Messianic Message of the Book of Mormon*, describes its purpose (Salt Lake City: Deseret Book, 1997). Elder Holland also devotes several pages to the theme of charity as taught by Mormon and Moroni. Hugh Nibley, too, touches briefly on this subject in his writings on the Book of Mormon.

4.   There are many important recurring themes in the Book of Mormon, including emphasis on the promises made to Israel, and on the Lord's purposes in establishing a land of promise. Not wishing, in any sense, to diminish those, I have obviously chosen a more limited focus here: the matter of charity and related subjects.

In revisiting the last several chapters of 2 Nephi, I am struck by the realization that Nephi's perspective at that point was in many ways similar to that of Mormon and Moroni. Why? In part because over the years he has seen pride and hatred grasp hearts among his own family and people, turning them onto destructive paths in the service of Satan. But we must remember that *a younger Nephi has also seen in vision what Mormon and Moroni experience in person, the annihilation of his people. And, like them, he has seen our day.* Having been shown the future—including details surrounding the birth and ministry of Jesus—through the miraculous lens of divine vision, Nephi has acquired the long perspective. It is that perspective we see in 2 Nephi 25–33, his closing chapters. And like Mormon and Moroni, in these chapters he speaks directly to us, to latter-day Israelites and Gentiles alike, warning us against the character flaws and foolish rejection of truth that would destroy his people and could well destroy us.

Of no small significance to my subject, however, is the portion of the younger Nephi's vision in which he sees the same things his father Lehi had seen. But Nephi's comprehension goes beyond his father's. As he ponders Lehi's words, Nephi is "caught away in the Spirit of the Lord," and he expresses a desire to see what his father saw. The first image the Spirit introduces is the tree that Lehi had beheld (1 Nephi 11:1–4), a tree of exceeding beauty "which is precious above all" (11:9).

The Spirit disappears, and an angel comes to instruct Nephi as to the meaning of the tree. That meaning is revealed through a vision of Mary cradling a baby in her arms. The angel identifies that baby as "the Lamb of God, yea, even the Son of the Eternal Father." Then immediately the angel asks Nephi if he knows now "the meaning of the tree," which is the tree of life. And Nephi knows. He says, "Yea, it is the love of God, which sheddeth itself abroad in the hearts of the children of men; wherefore, it is the most desirable above all things." And the angel replies, "Yea, and the most joyous to the soul" (11:21–23).

Ponder that revelation: the tree of life symbolizes "the love of God" manifest in mortal hearts, his love for us shown forth in our love for others. The pure love of Christ. Charity. Nephi goes on to say that he sees "the rod of iron" to be "the word of God," which word "leads to the fountain of living waters, or to the tree of life." Not only fountain, but also tree and rod, or word, Nephi learns, are "a representation of the love of God" (11:25). This is a testimony in itself of the value of the record, which is nothing less than the word of God. Have any of us fully realized that the Book of Mormon is a manifestation of God's love for us? His immense, limitless charity.

Early on, Nephi is taught what I am only now beginning to comprehend. He has come to know the indescribable beauty of a priceless concept that he and others would associate specifically with the word *charity*. He has come to understand the magnitude of the pure love of Christ. Later he would speak of the fruit of the tree in his vision as "the greatest of all the gifts of God" (1 Nephi 15:36). Surely Mormon, too, saw the connection between the word of God and pure divine love, the connection that became clear to Nephi through vision. Sadly enough, Nephi also knows that his people's hearts will harden, that love of both God and man, along with generosity and self-forgetfulness, will be driven out by anger, hate, and selfish pride. And he knows the result.

Nephi also sees in vision the cataclysm that will follow the Savior's death, obliterating cities in the promised land and destroying the more wicked among the Lehite people. He then gains further understanding of the "large and spacious building" his father had seen. Nephi sees the building that seems suspended in air with no foundation, just as most pride is based on thin air. He bears record that the "building was the pride of the world; and it fell, and the fall thereof was exceedingly great." The angel, with no little irony in his voice, says, "Behold the world and the wisdom thereof" (1 Nephi 11:35–36). That same angel alludes to the building yet again, underscoring what Nephi already knew, that it represents the "vain imaginations and the pride of the children of men" (1 Nephi 12:18). Pride, such as Nephi had already seen working in the hearts of Laman and Lemuel, is now addressed openly by a messenger from heaven. As the angel speaks, Nephi sees a final war between his posterity and the posterity of his rebellious brothers, a war in which his people are "overpower[ed] and "overcome" "because of pride . . . and the temptations of the devil" (12:19–20; see also vv. 18, 21).

The angel goes on to instruct Nephi regarding a still later day, a day when the "Gentiles" will inherit the land lost to his people but not entirely lost to his brothers' descendants. The angel speaks of a record coming forth one day among the Gentiles, a record written by Nephi's "seed" (see 1 Nephi 13 and 14). Having seen all these things, Nephi is exhausted, and heartbroken: "for I considered that mine afflictions were great above all, because of the destruction of my people, for I had beheld their fall" (1 Nephi 15:5). But there is a hopeful note. The "fulness of the gospel of the Messiah" will "come unto the Gentiles" in that future day, and from them the gospel will go "unto the remnant of our seed" (15:13), that is, to the Lamanites of the latter days.

The question was, and still is, what will we do with that great gospel gift that has come to us, embodied in the record, as Nephi foresaw it would? Will we foolishly lay it aside, ignore it, or seek to discredit it? Will we in our pride and vanity do as he foresees his people doing and wreak our own destruction, becoming the third great nation in the New World to forsake the divine promise of the land of promise? Truly, the fears and warnings of the first record keeper, Nephi, anticipate those of the last record keepers, Mormon and Moroni.

Like the last words of Mormon and Moroni, Nephi's last words sound a warning to people in the last days. And like Mormon and Moroni, Nephi lays a significant share of the blame for the destruction he foresees on the persistent pridefulness and lack of charity in his and succeeding generations. It is these stubborn sins and attitudes that cause people to deny Christ and fail to consecrate their lives to him in loving, humble worship.

Before offering his lengthy personal counsel, Nephi engraves more than a few of Isaiah's prophecies into the record. Many of these borrowings from the brass plates[5] prophesy of the Savior's birth, the scattering and gathering of Israel, the destruction that will precede the Second Coming, and also the millennial bliss that will follow. These are not the only prophecies Nephi records, however. In addition to lovely passages that foretell the establishment of "the Lord's house . . . in the top of the mountains" (2 Nephi 12:2; Isaiah 2:2) in the last days, Nephi includes Isaiah's words regarding things of great concern to Nephi—among them, a people inhabiting the promised land who are haughty and proud:

---

5. The brass plates, acquired with divine help and brought to the New World by Lehi's family, contained many writings that we today associate with the Old Testament, at least those writings prior to 600 BC. Possibly uncertain as to whether or not readers of his record would have access to these writings in their purity, an inspired Nephi engraved portions that he deemed essential for latter-day peoples.

Their land also is full of silver and gold, neither is there any end of their treasures; their land is also full of horses, neither is there any end of their chariots.[6]

Their land is also full of idols; they worship the work of their own hands, that which their own fingers have made.

And the mean [average] man boweth not down, and the great man humbleth himself not . . .[7]

And it shall come to pass that the lofty looks of man shall be humbled, and the haughtiness of men shall be bowed down. . . . (2 Nephi 12:7–11; Isaiah 2:7–11)

As candid as he is on the matter of pridefulness in these verses, Isaiah is ruthlessly frank in his description of latter-day women. He spends nine verses describing the abominable pride and self-display of "the daughters of Zion." Below is the opening verse of this particular condemnation, rendered in the Lord's words, a condemnation that follows hard upon the charge that "ye . . . grind the faces of the poor" (2 Nephi 13:15; Isaiah 3:15):

Moreover, the Lord saith: . . . the daughters of Zion are haughty, and walk with stretched-forth necks and wanton eyes, walking and mincing as they go, and making a tinkling with their feet— (2 Nephi 13:16; Isaiah 3:16)

We simply must realize that Nephi has a purpose in selecting these passages to preserve. Only the punctuation in these two verses varies from the King James Isaiah, and that just slightly. And Nephi preserves them, not on perishable material but on metal plates as part of the Nephite record that would be recovered and translated in our day. Note, too, that the reference is not to women of the world, but is specifically to women identified with the Lord's Kingdom, Zion. I cannot think the reference is limited to Jewish women. I, too, am a daughter of Zion. Again, the subject is the worldliness of pride, the opposite of humility.

In 2 Nephi 25, Nephi pauses to prophesy and speak powerfully of the coming Savior, whose earthly ministry he has seen in vision, and of whose infinite atonement he testifies. He also speaks at some length of the coming forth of the record at a later time. I can feel his concern as

---

6. Did Isaiah foresee motor vehicles?
7. The King James Bible omits the word *not* (twice) in this verse, which changes the meaning of the passage.

he addresses his people, calling them "a stiffnecked people," and warning them that his words will "stand as a testimony against you." Then he urges them, in language that speaks of consecration, to surrender the natural man and the worldly will to "the Holy One of Israel" and to "believe in Christ":

> Wherefore ye must bow down before him, and worship him with all your might, mind, and strength, and your whole soul. (2 Nephi 25:28–29)

This is humility. This is what true humility and consecration mean. This is what pure love of our Lord and Savior means. This is what Jesus himself taught when he walked the earth. The first great commandment. A commandment, as I observed above, that Jesus links inseparably to the second great commandment, love of neighbor or charity.

Nephi's pain is almost tangible in 2 Nephi 26 as he foresees the first great destructive episode in the future of his people, the cataclysm that will wrack the New World as a violent, cleansing sign of Jesus' crucifixion in the Old World. Nephi singles out "all those who are proud, and that do wickedly" (2 Nephi 26:4), as those who will suffer most in the first terrible event. The second event, the final destruction of his people, grieves Nephi to the very soul, because he has given his life to preserving them in faith. Yet here they are, the people he loves, heading toward irredeemable, complete destruction as "the reward of their pride and their foolishness." Instead of choosing the light, "they yield unto the devil and choose works of darkness" (26:10).

Nephi then moves in his prophecy to "the last days . . . when the Lord God shall bring these things forth unto the children of men" (26:14). By "these things" Nephi clearly means the Nephite record, "the words of the righteous" that "shall be written and sealed up in a book." This book, made by "those who shall be destroyed[,] shall speak unto them [latter-day peoples] out of the ground, . . . out of the dust" (26:15–17). What could be plainer than that? Anyone who doubts that a book is destined to come out of the ground in the last days, a book matching the description of the Book of Mormon and the plates from which the book would be translated, need only read Isaiah 29 (and 2 Nephi 27). Isaiah gives many details that fit undeniably with events surrounding the actual coming forth of the Book of Mormon.

Equally impressive is Nephi's pointed foreknowledge of our day.

He sees our time only too well. And what does he see and warn us against? Pridefulness, worldliness, and lack of charity. Even in our worship, he says, we have become worldly and prideful and selfish. Latter-day "gentiles are lifted up in the pride of their eyes," so much so that even though "they have built up many churches; nevertheless, they put down the power and miracles of God, and preach up unto themselves their own wisdom and their own learning." That is a powerful statement, and a damning one. Moreover, these things are done that the so-called preachers "may get gain and grind upon the face of the poor." As a result, instead of bringing love and harmony, the building up of "many churches . . . cause[s] envyings, and strifes, and malice" (2 Nephi 27:20–21).

Significantly, Nephi also foresees in our day "secret combinations" (2 Nephi 26:22), founded by the devil, that would not appear in Nephite society until generations later. Their goal is always power and wealth, and they play a major role in the downfall of both the Jaredite and Nephite societies. Nephi foresees, too, "priestcrafts" in which "men preach and set themselves up for a light unto the world." Their desire, regretfully, is not to bring people to Christ nor to instill faith and charity among their congregations, but to "get gain and praise of the world" for themselves. They have no interest in "the welfare of Zion" (26:29).

In stark contrast to the practices of these prideful, self-serving preachers are the teachings of the Lord himself. Nephi speaks plainly. Not only has "the Lord God forbidden this thing," but

> . . . the Lord God hath given a commandment that all men should have charity, which charity is love. And except they should have charity they were nothing. Wherefore, if they should have charity they would not suffer the laborer in Zion to perish. (26:30)

Repeatedly in chapter 26, Nephi describes the Lord as one whose primary desire is to bless the human family, "for he loveth the world." He denies none who come to him, and invites all to "partake of his goodness" because "all are alike unto God" (26:24–28, 33). This is the pure love of Christ which we are to emulate.

I find it interesting that in alluding here to some of the Ten Commandments, though not by name, Nephi describes a few of them in terms more closely identified with charity than are the terms in the original Decalogue. We readily recognize the injunctions against murdering, lying, stealing, taking the Lord's name in vain, and even committing "whoredoms." But Nephi uses plainer language in his similar listing of some of the things "the Lord hath commanded": mortals are not to "envy," nor to "have malice," nor to "contend one with another" (26:32). Nephi may have purposely chosen the word "envy" rather than "covet" and the phrase "have malice" rather than "bear false witness."

In any case, this subject greatly concerns Nephi, for it anticipates an immense weakness, even a fatal flaw, in modern society. In their wisdom, the ancients in some cultures identified pride as the deadliest of the Seven Deadly Sins. It comes first on the list, and with good reason. Pride leads to a host of other sins, and ultimately to destruction. Again in 2 Nephi 28, Nephi warns against false teachers in modern times. And again, he condemns them for their pride and the resultant demise of charity. Read with me several phrases and hear Nephi joining his voice with the Lord's:

> There shall be many which shall teach . . . false and vain and foolish doctrines, and shall be puffed up in their hearts . . .
>
> Because of pride, and because of false teachers, and false doctrine, their churches have become corrupted, and their churches are lifted up; because of pride they are puffed up.
>
> They rob the poor because of their fine sanctuaries; they rob the poor because of their fine clothing; and they persecute the meek and the poor in heart, because in their pride they are puffed up.
>
> They wear stiff necks and high heads; . . . they have all gone astray save it be a few, who are the humble followers of Christ; nevertheless, they are led, that in many instances they do err because they are taught by the precepts of men.
>
> O the wise, and the learned, and the rich, that are puffed up in the pride of their hearts, . . . wo, wo, wo be unto them, saith the Lord God Almighty. . . . (2 Nephi 28:9, 12–15)

The last verses of chapter 28 and all of chapter 29 speak directly to people in our day who willfully belittle and dismiss the Book of Mormon. More powerful testimony of that book could not be born as Nephi quotes the Lord directly, from 2 Nephi 28:30 through 29:13. I urge anyone not yet convinced of the truth and importance of the Book of Mormon—whether a member of The Church of Jesus Christ of Latter-day Saints or not—to read those revelations slowly and prayerfully. They are intended for us, and they are in the Lord's own voice.

Most assuredly, we "wear stiff necks and high heads" at our eternal peril.

Chapter 31 is a beautiful treatise on the doctrine of Christ, an encouraging discourse in which Nephi entreats us to "endure to the end in following the example of the Son of the living God" (2 Nephi 31:16). Here he sounds a note of great hope if we will but do that. (The statement also sheds light on what constitutes enduring to the end.) I quote one lovely verse in its entirety but ask you to pay special heed to the words in italics, words we sometimes overlook in our well-justified enthusiasm for the rest of the passage.

> Wherefore, ye must press forward with a steadfastness in Christ, having a perfect brightness of hope, *and a love of God and of all men*. Wherefore, if ye shall press forward, feasting upon the word of Christ, and endure to the end, behold, thus saith the Father: Ye shall have eternal life. (31:20, emphasis added)

There it is in a nutshell, the key to attaining eternal life: faith, hope, charity (love of God and neighbor), and endurance in all three—aided immensely by not merely reading but by *feasting* on Christ's revealed word. Most especially the Book of Mormon.

In these chapters an obviously inspired Nephi is so intent on both warning us and showing us the glorious possibilities that await us—if we "will enter in by the way, and receive the Holy Ghost,"and follow its promptings (2 Nephi 32:5)—that the Spirit has to constrain him. Unable to say more about these sacred matters, he is left, as he says, "to mourn," not only because of men's "unbelief," "wickedness," and "ignorance," but also because of their "stiffneckedness." They refuse to "search knowledge," much less to "understand great knowledge, when it is given unto them in plainness" (32:7), as it is in the Book of Mormon. That word "stiffneckedness" is not a word we are accustomed to using in twenty-first century English, but it appears repeatedly in the Book of Mormon, along with phrases like "puffed up," to create an unforgettable image of pride.

And now we arrive at 2 Nephi 33, Nephi's concluding words to future generations. As I reread it, I am struck again by the sheer power of his testimony. This chapter, along with passages in Ether 12 and Moroni 10, should be in everyone's heart and on everyone's tongue. This great man and prophet knows whereof he speaks. And what does he say before he bears final testimony? Read these words:

> I have charity for my people, and great faith in Christ that I shall meet many souls spotless at his judgment-seat.
>
> I have charity for the Jew—I say Jew, because I mean them from whence I came.
>
> I also have charity for the Gentiles. But behold, for none of these can I hope except they shall be reconciled unto Christ, and enter into the narrow gate, and walk in the strait path which leads to life, and continue in the path until the end of the day of probation. (2 Nephi 33:7–9)

Three times Nephi uses the word "charity," though he might have simply said, "I have charity for my people, for the Jew, and for the Gentile." But he didn't. He very deliberately repeats the phrase "I have charity," giving it special emphasis in these, his last words, not only to "my beloved brethren, and also Jew," but also to "all ye ends of the earth" (33:13). He is a man of charity, a man of humility and pure love, and he wants us to know that about him. He also wants us to know that Christ lives and has taught him personally. And he wants us to know that the record is true, that it carries the word of Christ.

I simply cannot leave Nephi's closing words to us without including his stirring testimony of the record he has kept and that others after him will continue to keep. "Hearken unto these words," he says, "and believe in Christ." Furthermore, he insists that we cannot believe in Christ without believing these words, because "he hath given them unto me" (33:10). Read his testimony aloud and then try to tell me this is not a living man speaking, a prophet of the living God:

> And if they [the words I have written] are not the words of Christ, judge ye—for Christ will show unto you, with power and great glory, that they are his words, at the last day; and you and I shall stand face to face before his bar; and ye shall know that I have been commanded of him to write these things, notwithstanding my weakness. (33:11)

What could be more moving, and more frightening too, as Nephi both testifies and warns every mortal creature, "all ye ends of the earth"? He speaks, he says, "as the voice of one crying from the dust" (33:13). These are his closing words:

And you that will not partake of the goodness of God, and respect the words of the Jews [the Bible], and also my words, and the words which shall proceed out of the mouth of the Lamb of God, behold, I bid you an everlasting farewell, for these words shall condemn you at the last day.

For what I seal on earth, shall be brought against you at the judgment bar; for thus hath the Lord commanded me, and I must obey. Amen. (33:14–15)

It is out of love for us, as he says, that he makes the record, that he fashions metal plates and engraves them, through every imaginable difficulty—and this while carrying the responsibility for the very life and continued existence of his nation and people. It is out of love for us that he urges and enjoins and pleads with us to feast on these words, for they are the saving words of Christ. It is out of love for us that Nephi virtually commands us to come to our Lord and Savior, Jesus Christ, the Son of God. It is out of love that he warns us against the pitfalls of pride and ambition and unkindness.

This is a man whose life was the very essence of charity, the very embodiment of pure love. I testify with all energy of mind and heart, nothing doubting, nothing wavering, that like Mormon and Moroni and all the prophets in between, Nephi lived and loved and wrote. Truly, he was a man of God; he spoke with angels and he heard the voice of his Lord. This I know with every ounce of my being. This I pray that you, too, will know.

II

IN NEPHI'S FOOTSTEPS: JACOB AND ENOS

Although Nephi has consecrated both Jacob and Joseph as "priests and teachers over the land of my people" (2 Nephi 5:26), it is Jacob who is to be the spiritual leader of the Nephite people after Nephi is gone. He will not, however, serve in the role of king. Jacob seems a quieter, more contemplative, less dynamic sort of fellow than his older brother; but Nephi assures us, indirectly perhaps, that Jacob is a spiritual power-house and equal to the task. Nephi sends this message by inserting one of Jacob's sermons into his own record. Nephi knows that Jacob will be given charge of the record one day, that he will include writings of his own, but Nephi wants to assure that this particular sermon will be preserved for future generations. It acquires the prominence of Nephi's final words and, except for several Isaiah chapters that Nephi copies into the record, immediately precedes Nephi's closing admonitions to his readers. It is splendid.

Significantly, in the verses just before the Jacob sermon, Nephi speaks of the fact that the Lord has told him to make another set of plates, a set devoted to "the things of God." These new plates are to be a companion set to the plates given essentially to "the history of my people" (2 Nephi 5:30–33). That Nephi would place this sermon where he does, almost in response to the Lord's injunction to keep a separate *sacred* record, gives it added importance in my mind. It also appears that Nephi has asked Jacob to deliver this particular sermon, or at least to make certain writings of Isaiah part of it (see 2 Nephi 6:4). And Jacob does read from Isaiah, chapters 50–51, and a few verses from chapters 49 and 52, before launching into his own remarkable address.

Like Nephi, Jacob has a direct link to heaven, for he has been taught by angels (see 2 Nephi 6:9; 10:3; Jacob 7:5) and by the Lord himself (see 2 Nephi 11:3; Jacob 7:5). This lengthy sermon is not delivered in one day, but is split into two parts. And even then, Nephi does not attempt to preserve it all. He says that "Jacob spake many more things to my people at that time; nevertheless only these things have I caused to be written" (2 Nephi 11:1). Most of chapter 9 reports the section of Jacob's sermon devoted to the Atonement of "the Holy One of Israel" (2 Nephi 9:15) and its eternal implications. It is one of the finest discourses on the infinite Atonement ever delivered by a mortal, and I urge you to pore over it and absorb it

Of particular interest to my subject just now—and I think of particular interest to Nephi as he moves toward his own last words of warning and counsel—are the words Jacob speaks as he concludes his discourse on the Atonement. Verse 27 of 2 Nephi 9 serves as a transition from brilliant doctrinal discourse to resolute warning, spoken to a beloved people. Jacob fears greatly for his people, and he knows what awaits them if they do not humble themselves in the bonds of faith, brotherhood, and charity. I suggest that you read this section of Jacob's sermon (2 Nephi 9:28–54), and chapter 10 also, alongside Nephi's closing chapters. The two passages seem to flow together in a joint expression of concern for later as well as present generations. You might also want to read the Isaiah chapters quoted by Jacob with those inserted by Nephi.

Jacob holds nothing back as he cries "wo unto" the person "like unto us" who has the law and the commandments and does not heed them (9:27). Then he launches into a rhetorical exhortation against pride and self-satisfaction:

> . . . O the vainness, and the frailties, and the foolishness of men! When they are learned they think they are wise, and they hearken not unto the counsel of God, for they set it aside, supposing they know of themselves, wherefore, their wisdom is foolishness and it profiteth them not. And they shall perish. (9:28)

Jacob tosses in a caveat, however, lest anyone use him as an excuse to avoid education: "But to be learned is good if they hearken unto the counsels of God" (9:29).

Jacob next warns those "who are rich as to the things of the world," for worldly riches can dull one's charitable instincts. The rich, he says, are too often prone to "despise the poor, and . . . persecute the meek." Moreover, "their hearts are upon their treasures; wherefore, their treasure is their god. And behold, their treasure shall perish with them also" (9:30). Jacob further evokes "wo unto" the prideful "deaf that will not hear," the "blind that will not see," the "uncircumcised of heart," and a whole host of others (9:31–38). Without humble repentance, all such are doomed to perish. Repeatedly he pleads, "O, my beloved brethren," begging them to heed his counsel and thereby qualify to enter the gate of "the Holy One of Israel" (9:39–41). Yet, again he warns the prideful learned and wealthy:

> The wise, and the learned, and they that are rich, who are puffed up because of their learning, and their wisdom, and their riches— yea, they are they whom he despiseth; and save they shall cast these things away, and consider themselves fools before God, and come down in the depths of humility, he will not open unto them. (9:42)

Then Jacob adopts a more personal tone, pleading with his people to cast off their sins and partake of the grace and mercy of the Lord. On that sweeter note, he concludes for the day, but tells his listeners that he has more instruction for them "on the morrow" (9:54). That very night Jacob learns from an angel that the name of the coming Messiah is "Christ" (2 Nephi 10:3). Jacob is apparently the first mortal of record to know that name. This, in itself, tells me how this humble Nephite prophet is regarded in divine counsels. His heartfelt care and fear for his people is an undeniable manifestation of the pure love of Christ. It is no wonder Nephi made this sermon of his younger brother part of his own final warning and promise to us in a later day.

Jacob begins the book bearing his name with the instructions handed to him by Nephi regarding the two sets of records, the sacred and the historical. He also pays tribute to his brother, who was the much loved leader of the Nephite people. Jacob includes in his book a sermon he delivered "after the death of Nephi" (Jacob 2:1), though we don't know how long after. The Jacob we see in this sermon is a sorrowful man, obviously burdened with an overwhelming sense of the responsibility that now rests on his shoulders. We also see a very tenderhearted, humble, caring man—a man who does not welcome the necessity to speak to his people about their sins. He says quite frankly, "I this day am weighed down with much more desire and anxiety for the welfare of your souls than I have hitherto been" (2:3). Jacob is a man who is now able to feel and fully express the pure love of Christ.

Repeatedly he speaks of being grieved at the message he has been divinely commissioned to deliver, mainly to the men in his congregation, "concerning the wickedness of your hearts" (2:6). He is particularly aware of the "exceedingly tender and chaste and delicate" feelings of their wives and children (2:7). There is a sweetness and humility about Jacob that touches my heart as I sense how difficult this assignment is for him. Nonetheless, he obeys, for the Lord spoke to him "saying: Jacob, get thou up into the temple on the morrow, and declare the word which I shall give thee unto this people" (2:11).

Later Jacob will speak of the moral digressions of the Nephite men, but his first subject (i.e., the Lord's first subject) is pride and lack of charity. He notes that many have "begun to search for gold, and for silver, and for all manner of precious ores" (2:12), and that they have been blessed with riches. But, unfortunately,

> . . . because some of you have obtained more abundantly than that of your brethren ye are lifted up in the pride of your hearts, and wear stiff necks and high heads because of the costliness of your apparel, and persecute your brethren because ye suppose that ye are better than they. (2:13)

Jacob goes on to warn his people against supposing that God will justify this kind of behavior. In fact, God condemns it, and if they persist in it, they will experience his harsh judgments. Jacob pleads with them:

> O that ye would listen unto the words of [God's] commands, and let not this pride of your hearts destroy your souls.
>
> Think of your brethren like unto yourselves, and be familiar with all and free with your substance, that they may be rich like unto you.
>
> But before ye seek for riches, seek ye for the kingdom of God. (2:16–18)

If you do so, he says, you may well find riches, but you will find riches only if you seek them "for the intent to do good—to clothe the naked, and to feed the hungry, and to liberate the captive, and administer relief to the sick and the afflicted" (2:19).

This is the Lord speaking through his prophet, and he is speaking of charity, virtually commanding the exercise of pure love. Jacob is ready, now, to turn to an even more difficult subject, but he issues these final warnings against the sin of pride:

> Those of you which have afflicted your neighbor, and persecuted him because ye were proud in your hearts, of the things which God hath given you, what say ye of it?
>
> Do ye not suppose that such things are abominable unto him who created all flesh? And the one being is as precious in his sight as the other. And all flesh is of the dust. . . . (2:20–21)

Jacob then, though it burdens him, speaks the Lord's words condemning the whoredoms that are occupying some Nephite men. The Lord grieves especially, as does Jacob, over the sorrow and suffering this abomination visits on faithful wives and children. Jacob also speaks encouragingly to the "pure in heart," urging them to "receive the pleasing word of God, and feast upon his love," which they can do if their "minds are firm, forever" (3:2).

I move now to words that read very much like those of a man nearing the end of his ministry as well as the end of his record. Jacob seems to begin his conclusion in chapter 4, but being "led on the by Spirit unto prophesying" (Jacob 4:15), he repeats the lengthy allegory of the olive tree (see Jacob 5) from the writings of Zenos.[1] In Jacob 6 he interprets the allegory. I note, too, that by way of introducing the Zenos allegory, Jacob returns to the subject of pride—this time among the Jews, they who would reject their own promised Messiah:

> But behold, the Jews were a stiffnecked people; and they despised the words of plainness, and killed the prophets, and sought for things that they could not understand. Wherefore, because of their blindness, which blindness came by looking beyond the mark, they must needs fall; for God hath taken away his plainness from them, and delivered unto them many things which they cannot understand . . . that they may stumble. (Jacob 4:14)

---

1. The writings of Zenos were apparently in the brass plates which Lehi's family brought from Jerusalem. As with some other writings cited by Book of Mormon prophets, these do not appear in our Bible today. Presumably, they are among the many "plain and precious things" that an angel told Nephi had been lost or deleted from the Old Testament record (see 1 Nephi 13).

Always, always, pride is a subject of great concern among Nephite prophets, and it becomes an important cautionary theme in their final recorded words. And always, the antidote to pride is humility and charity, the pure love of Christ.

Before ending his record, Jacob describes his encounter with a prideful anti-Christ named Sherem (see Jacob 7). After finally confessing to his lies, Sherem "gave up the ghost" (Jacob 7:20). The astonished Nephites, "overcome" by "the power of God," sink to the earth (7:21). Significantly, "the love of God was restored again among" them, and they become more steady in the faith (7:23). Jacob also speaks of the importance of the record to succeeding generations and testifies fervently of Christ and the power of his word. And again he bears witness of the Atonement and the Resurrection.

I am forever haunted by an aged Jacob's closing words. They are the words of a man who has suffered much, who has felt the burden of leadership through both peaceful and fearful times, who has become the very essence of meekness and lowliness of heart. Read his words aloud and know him; this man felt his exile deeply and knew his total dependence on the Lord:

> I conclude this record . . . by saying that the time passed away with us, and also our lives passed away like as it were unto us a dream, we being a lonesome and a solemn people, wanderers, cast out from Jerusalem, born in tribulation, in a wilderness, and hated of our brethren, which caused wars and contentions; wherefore, we did mourn out our days. (7:26).

"We did mourn out our days." That one phrase speaks volumes. I mourn today with my dear brother Jacob whom I have grown to love.

Jacob's legacy was not to be lost, at least not immediately. He turns the record over to his son Enos, who must have been trustworthy or Jacob would not have done this, nor would this good son have willingly accepted the responsibility (see 7:27). Enos remembers the teachings of his father and goes humbly before the Lord, praying ceaselessly all day and into the night. Then, having received a remission of his own sins, Enos's heart turns in pure love to his Nephite and Lamanite brothers and sisters. He "pour[s] out" his "whole soul" for them (Enos 1:9, 11), begging the Lord to extend mercy and redemption to them. He also thinks of us and beseeches the Lord to preserve the record for "some future day" (1:13), to bless later generations.

We are sometimes prone to dismiss Enos too quickly. Perhaps the brevity of his record leads us to regard him as an habitual sinner who finally repents. Actually, we don't know that his sins were exceptionally serious. We remember that Nephi, too, was burdened by a sense of his unworthiness and sins (see 2 Nephi 4:17–19, 27, 32). I suspect that we are seeing just a glimpse here of an unusually humble man who judges himself and his actions by a very high standard. To see the real Enos, the man of immense charity, we need to consider how earnestly he prayed for forgiveness and how deep his faith went.

Enos's writings are not lengthy, but he has observed a lack of charity among the Nephites in even this, the second generation. They "were a stiffnecked people," he says, "hard [i.e., unwilling] to understand" (Enos 1:22). Any who doubt that Enos is a chosen emissary of God, an inspired prophet, need only read the last two verses of his record, written as he nears death. Here is a man who has risen to meet his challenges. I find it quite amazing that where his father was sorrowful and downcast in the end, Enos is celebratory and confident, having declared "the truth which is in Christ . . . all my days, and . . . rejoiced in it above that of the world" (1:26). His concluding statement reminds me of Moroni, who finished a life of trial in an explosion of triumphant faith. Hear Enos:

> And I soon go to the place of my rest, which is with my Redeemer; for I know that in him I shall rest. And I rejoice in the day when my mortal shall put on immortality, and shall stand before him; then shall I see his face with pleasure, and he will say unto me, ye blessed, there is a place prepared for you in the mansions of my Father. Amen. (1:27)

Glorious. Need I say more?

PART TWO

MOMENTS OF GRACE, *Christ's Love* SHOWERED ON *Earth*

I

THE BROTHER OF JARED: AN EARLY VISION

The earliest of what I am calling "moments of grace" comes not in the Nephite record, but in Moroni's abridgement of the book of Ether. The very fact that the beginning of the Jaredite nation, in the vicinity of 2200 BC, far pre-dates the inception of Lehite-Nephite civilization has led me to give brief special attention to one particular incident. Rather than attempt to blend it into the Nephite record, I have chosen to include it here and to set it apart, just as a rare and precious jewel might be separated out from others of a much later date. My hope is that this incredible event will set the tone for what follows after.

Anyone familiar with the Book of Mormon knows about the great prophet whom the record identifies only as the brother of Jared. He is the spiritual leader of the band of Israelites who were directed to leave their Old World dwellings at the time of the Tower of Babel and the confusing of tongues. After a period of preparation in the desert, they were brought in closed boats, by the hand of the Lord, to the New World, the promised land. The incident I wish to mention here is amazing and it clearly serves as a supreme moment, outside of time, for Moroni, who abridged the record of these people. The Lord himself first speaks to the brother of Jared, and then he visits him in a cloud, at least twice. Then, wonder of wonders, the Lord appears before this stunned man in his full spiritual embodiment, in form the same as the mortal body in which he will minister on earth. We have to remember that at this period in history very probably the only major prophets to have preceded this man, other than Adam, were Enoch and Noah. *This is early.*

The brother of Jared has found sixteen small stones that he asks the Lord to "touch . . . with thy finger, and prepare them that they may shine forth in darkness" and light the eight vessels that are to carry his people across the sea (Ether 3:4). In answer to the man's fervent prayer, "the veil was taken from off the eyes of the brother of Jared, and he saw the finger of the Lord; and it was as the finger of a man, like unto flesh and blood" (3:6). He collapses in fright, realizing for the first time that the Lord looks like a man. The Lord then makes a rather astounding statement: "Because of thy faith thou hast seen that I shall take upon me flesh and blood; and never has man come before me with such exceeding faith as thou hast" (3:9). This man has shown more faith than any man prior to this time. And then, encouraged by the Lord's subsequent question, the man says, "Lord, show thyself unto me" (3:10).

After questioning the brother of Jared further, "the Lord showed himself unto him, and said: Because thou knowest these things ye are redeemed from the fall; therefore ye are brought back into my presence; therefore I show myself unto you" (3:13). So great is the faith of the brother of Jared that his redemption is already promised. Then the Lord declares boldly and unequivocally who he is:

> Behold, I am he who was prepared from the foundation of the world to redeem my people. Behold, I am Jesus Christ. I am the Father and the Son. In me shall all mankind have life, and that eternally, even they who shall believe on my name; and they shall become my sons and my daughters. (3:14)[1]

It is obvious that Moroni is deeply impressed by the miraculous visitation of the Lord to his ancient prophet, and by that prophet's extraordinary faith. Moroni retells the event, in his own words this time, words full of awe and wonder. It is as though he cannot bear to let go of this sacred experience but must rehearse it to clarify it in his mind. Still, the wonders do not cease even now, for not only does the

---

1. Pause for just a moment on the statement that Christ is both Father and Son. At first glance, this could seem to suggest that Father and Son are one rather than two separate beings. The Lord's next statement seems to clarify the matter. In using the phrase "who shall believe," he says, in essence, that mortals who truly accept him as their Redeemer are reborn spiritually as his spiritual offspring. There are ample confirmations of this truth in the books of Mosiah and Alma (see Index under "Born of God").

Lord come in person to this man, but he shows him a marvelous vision of "all the inhabitants of the earth which had been, and also all that would be; and he withheld them not from his sight, even unto the ends of the earth" (3:25).

Still enlivened by the Spirit after writing of this holy occurrence, Moroni goes on to describe the particular instance of the Lord's speaking directly to him on these and other matters. The Lord is very specific about the recording of these sacred events and the subsequent handling of the record of them, which record, he says, "shall not go forth unto the Gentiles until the day that they shall repent of their iniquity, and become clean before the Lord" (Ether 4:6). It is a powerful moment as the Lord makes it very clear to Moroni, and to us, just who he is and what lies in store at his hand if we prove worthy. He identifies himself as "Jesus Christ; . . . I am he who speaketh" (4:8). His words leap off the page, words delivered with divine authority and clear intent:

> And at my command the heavens are opened and are shut; and at my word the earth shall shake; and at my command the inhabitants thereof shall pass away, even so as by fire . . .
>
> But he that believeth these things which I have spoken, him will I visit with the manifestations of my Spirit, and he shall know and bear record . . .
>
> And whatsoever thing persuadeth men to do good is of me; for good cometh of none save it be of me. I am the same that leadeth men to all good; he that will not believe my words will not believe me—that I am; and he that will not believe me will not believe the Father who sent me. For behold, I am the Father, I am the light, and the life, and the truth of the world. (4:9, 11–12)

And then the Lord makes a promise to us if we will come to him: "Come unto me, O ye Gentiles, and I will show unto you the greater things, the knowledge which is hid up because of unbelief" (4:13).

As you ponder the words of Christ to the brother of Jared and to Moroni, let your mind embrace the fact that he is the source of pure love that we extend to others. Remember that he said, "whatsoever thing persuadeth men to do good is of me" (4:12).

II

BENJAMIN

Although I inserted a short segment from the book of Ether, by way of introduction to the second part of this volume, we are not quite finished with "last words" of Nephite prophets. My main purpose in these pages, however, is to rejoice with you at accounts of charity and pure love in action among the Nephite and Lamanite peoples. We will see conversions so glorious that heaven seems to have taken up residence on earth. We will see hearts changed and lives turned in full and lasting consecration to the Lord's work. With some reluctance, however, I add a small disclaimer. The thrilling moments of conversion and miracles and the outpouring of love among God's children are truly full of wonder and peace while their effects last, but they are never sustained indefinitely. All too soon, especially among the Nephite peoples, pride, selfishness, and a craving for power and riches signal the rejection of charity and pure love. Be that as it may, we can relish the lovely moments of grace when we witness changed hearts and God's hand blessing his children.

King Benjamin's closing address to his people, which Mormon inscribed into the record in its entirety, makes a splendid bridge into that beatific realm. It contains, as the great British poet and essayist, Matthew Arnold, insists all great literature must, both instruction and delight. Although we are introduced to Benjamin in Omni and the Words of Mormon, we actually see and hear the man Benjamin in only the first six chapters of the book of Mosiah, this Mosiah being the son who succeeds him on the throne. Benjamin is an old man now, having achieved a hard-won peace on the battlefield, and he gives counsel to his sons and a charge concerning the records. His final words to his people, whom he has called together in a vast assemblage at the temple, begin in chapter 2. This address, and the response of his listeners, is one of the high points in all scripture for me. I urge you to absorb it and be transformed, as Benjamin's people were transformed. Mosiah 2 through 5 will touch you deeply if you let the words sink into your mind and soul. Chapters 2, 4, and 5 come right from Benjamin's great heart and his incredible humility. Chapter 3 comes directly from heaven in words delivered to Benjamin by an angel sent from God himself (Mosiah 3:2, 23).

What Benjamin and the angel teach the Nephite throngs is as important to us today as it was to the people of that long-ago time. Man and angel testify in elevated language of the coming Lord Omnipotent and his atoning, saving sacrifice for earth's children. And they teach charity in its every manifestation—humility, love, service, selflessness, patience, forgiveness, gratitude, and more. Again, I marvel that the last words of so many Book of Mormon prophets and leaders carry that same counsel. The miracle of Benjamin's sermon is that his message of faith in Christ, and the pure love that is charity, leads to an almost indescribable moment of divine grace. The people's hearts are changed; they are spiritually reborn as sons and daughters of the Lord Jesus Christ.[1] This is the first of several lovely, incredible, even magical, moments of true conversion in the Book of Mormon, and we will visit

---

1. I mentioned earlier that in the 179th Semi-annual Conference of the Church in October 2009, speaker after speaker urged us to love one another, to unite in love and faith. President Henry B. Eyring, first counselor to President Thomas S. Monson, was one who touched many hearts with that message. "Our way of life, hour by hour," he said, "must be filled with the love of God and love for others." He spoke also of the sorrow that "comes primarily from selfishness, which is the absence of love" (*Ensign*, Nov. 2009, 70, 71). He might well have said absence of charity. Clearly, the subject of charity was on President Eyring's mind because he had focused on it in the Relief Society session of General Conference just a week earlier. In that address he connected charity with a change of heart, just as the sensitive reader of Benjamin's address and the subsequent change in his listeners would see that inevitable connection. "Charity is born of faith in the Lord Jesus Christ and is an effect of His Atonement working in the hearts of the members," President Eyring said. He added further that "feelings of charity spring from hearts changed" (*Ensign*, Nov. 2009, 121).

some of them in succession as we move to the lovely fruits of warnings and counsel heeded.

It is clear that Benjamin, while he was king of the Nephite people, became the keeper of all the Nephite records when an aging Amaleki passed them to him (see Omni 1:25; Words of Mormon 1:10). Apparently no consistent pattern had been established for delivering the plates from one person or generation to the next, though it was often from brother to brother, father to son, or ruler to ruler. What is consistent throughout Nephite history, from Benjamin's time on, is the handing of records to a born leader and prophet, "a just man before the Lord," as Amaleki said of Benjamin (Omni 1:25), whether king or not. What is less clear is whether or not Benjamin added to the larger record himself. It seems logical to assume that he did, though perhaps briefly, because Mormon is able to summarize Benjamin's era and accomplishments rather quickly (see Words of Mormon 1:12–18). Near the end of his life, Benjamin passes both crown and records to his son Mosiah.

By anyone's standard, Benjamin was a remarkable man and a remarkable magistrate. He managed to unite his people and lead them, in person, to victory against their enemies. He also rid them of false Christs, false prophets, and false teachers. Moreover, with the help of prophets, he was able to bring peace out of contention and dissent among a people who had been prideful and difficult to govern. "Stiff-necked" is the term Mormon uses to describe their malady (1:17).

I sense that the multitudes who gather at the temple to hear their king are not a wicked bunch of rebellious apostates, but are a people who probably regard themselves as believers yet they have grown somewhat ungrateful and careless in their religious observances. They have become self-serving, neglectful, and unkind to the less fortunate. In short, they have set aside the two great commandments—to love God and each other. They have become wrapped up in things of the world, and they have failed in charity. Benjamin's entire address is given not to chastise his people for murderous, thieving, or unchaste behavior, but rather to entreat them to live on a higher plane. He wants them to rise above petty selfishness and pride, to open their hearts to God and to others.

Benjamin's opening words make it clear that his concern for the character of his people and their ultimate welfare is genuine and runs deep. He has not commanded them to gather "to trifle with the words" he will speak but to "open your ears that ye may hear, and your hearts that ye may understand, and your minds that the mysteries of God may be unfolded to your view" (Mosiah 2:9). Benjamin sets the tone for the occasion by reminding his people that he has not placed himself above them but has regarded himself as one of them, one whose office and calling has been to serve them.

He has not used his position to acquire wealth or to live off the labor of others. Standing before an ancient people as well as before us on the page is a selfless and humble monarch, one who strives to be the example of service and humility he wishes his people to emulate. Twice he declares that his intent in saying these things is not to boast but to teach. Boasting is beneath this noble king. His heartfelt desire, his last and lasting wish for his people, is that they "learn wisdom," that they learn "that when ye are in the service of your fellow beings ye are only in the service of your God" (2:17).

Building on the unequivocal directive that his people serve one another, Benjamin reminds them, in the strongest words he can muster, that it is God to whom they owe thanks, more than to their earthly king. Benjamin pursues this theme in great earnestness and at some length. Here is a brief sample of his utterance:

> If you should render all the thanks and praise which your whole soul has the power to possess, to that God who has created you, and has kept and preserved you, and has caused that ye should rejoice, . . .
>
> [Even] lending you breath, that ye may live and move and do according to your own will, and even supporting you from one moment to another—I say, if ye should serve him with all your whole souls yet ye would be unprofitable servants.
>
> And behold, all that he requires of you is to keep his commandments. . . . (2:20–22)

A small price to pay. And the specific commandments Benjamin is speaking of on this auspicious occasion are the two on which hang all the law and the prophets, love of God and love of neighbor. The pure love of Christ. Charity.

Thus, service, humility, and obedience to divine commandments are the themes Benjamin emphasizes as he prepares his people to hear words of instruction from the angelic emissary, instruction about the coming Savior of the world. Benjamin also reminds his listeners that they are forever in God's debt because his blessings multiply as mortal gratitude and service are extended. "Therefore," Benjamin asks, "of what have ye to boast?" (2:24). Should any be inclined to think too well of themselves, he advises humility: "Ye cannot say that ye are even as much as the dust of the earth; but behold, it belongeth to him who created you" (2:25). And should any suppose that Benjamin thinks too well of himself, he disabuses them of the notion: "And I, even I, whom ye call your king, am no better than ye yourselves are; for I am also of the dust" (2:26).

As he prepares his people to hear heaven-sent words, Benjamin warns them against engaging in contentions and giving heed to "the evil spirit." Were they to rebel openly against God and fail to repent, they would be consigning themselves to "a never-ending torment" (2:32, 33, 37–39). Remember your eternal indebtedness to "your Heavenly Father," he says, and "render to him all that you have and are" (2:34). Let his Spirit "guide you in wisdom's paths" (2:36) so that you will keep his commandments and thereby "be blessed in all things." I can hear the urgency in Benjamin's voice as he cries, "O remember, remember that these things are true; for the Lord has spoken it" (2:41).

In chapter 3, it is Benjamin's voice that is heard, but the words recorded are those of the messenger angel, sent specifically to instruct these Nephites who have been drifting spiritually. Twice the angel utters the word "joy," and again the word "rejoice," as he describes the Lord's desire for his people's happiness (see Mosiah 3:3–4). But it is a joy purchased at no small cost, for the Lord, the very Creator, will come to earth as a man, to suffer "more than man can suffer, except it be unto death" (3:7) in order to redeem mortal men. Over the centuries, "the Lord God saw that his people were a stiffnecked" bunch whose hearts were "hardened" (3:14–15). Because of their willful pride, they were given the Law of Moses, a law of performances. But they failed to see "that the law of Moses availeth nothing except it were through the atonement of his blood" (3:15). Bearing strong testimony that salvation comes only through Christ, the angel then speaks even more directly to Benjamin's listeners.

He warns that "men drink damnation to their own souls except they humble themselves and become as little children," believing in salvation through "the atoning blood of Christ" (3:18). The angel says emphatically that "the natural man is an enemy to God, and has been since the fall of Adam, and will be, forever and ever, unless he yields to the enticings of the Holy Spirit, and putteth off the natural man and becometh a saint through the atonement of Christ the Lord." And how does one put off the natural man and become a saint? The angel does not leave us guessing on the matter. To be worthy of the Atonement's transforming powers, one must "[become] as a child, submissive, meek, humble, patient, full of love, willing to submit to all things which the Lord seeth fit to inflict upon him" (3:19). Do those qualities sound familiar? Yes, indeed. To be worthy of the Atonement's transforming powers, one becomes, in essence, a person of charity.

Lest any should mistake the source of his words, the angel says, "And thus saith the Lord: They [the words spoken] shall stand as a bright testimony against this people at the judgment day" (3:24). And because we have received these words also, we are likewise accountable for them.

The heavenly message strikes home. This is a compelling moment of realization for Benjamin's people, a moment of new insight and devastating self-knowledge. But what needed to happen does happen. Their hearts are opened to the Spirit; they have looked into their own souls. They see what they have been and know what they must become. Pride melts away, and they are humbled. This selfish, stiffnecked people fall "to the earth, for the fear of the Lord ha[s] come upon them." They have "viewed themselves in their own carnal state, even less than the dust of the earth." They cry out for mercy and forgiveness, asking that Christ's atoning blood purify their hearts. They testify of their belief "in Jesus Christ, the Son of God, who created heaven and earth, and all things; who shall come down among the children of men" (Mosiah 4:1–2).

Their pleas are heard, and "the Spirit of the Lord came upon them, and they were filled with joy, having received a remission of their sins" (4:3). Benjamin then begins instructing his people in a deeply affecting way, reminding them repeatedly that they have no cause to be other than entirely humble and steady in faith. The language in which he now addresses them, and the emphasis he places on humility, leave no room for misunderstanding. Man is nothing compared to God, and he should not forget that—ever. Thus, the first section of Benjamin's message, after he witnesses the heart-changing experience of repentance and conversion among his people, is on the subject of humility. He does not want his people to lose or forget what they have experienced, and he uses language that cannot be misunderstood:

He implies that "the knowledge of the goodness of God" should have "awakened you to a sense of your nothingness, and your worthless and fallen state—" (4:5). He virtually commands his hearers to "believe in God; believe that he is, and that he created all things, both in heaven and in earth; believe that he has all wisdom, and all power, both in heaven and in earth," and to "believe that man doth not comprehend all the things which the Lord can comprehend" (4:9). "Repent . . . and humble yourselves before God," and ask for forgiveness, Benjamin says, and again he speaks pointedly: "If you believe all these things see that ye do them" (4:10).

In verse 11 Benjamin reiterates and summarizes the heart of his message thus far:

> As ye have come to the knowledge of the glory of God, or if ye have known of his goodness and have tasted of his love, . . . even so I would that ye should remember, and always retain in remembrance, the greatness of God, and your own nothingness, and his goodness and long-suffering towards you, unworthy creatures, and humble yourselves even in the depths of humility, calling on the name of the Lord daily, and standing steadfastly in the faith of that which is to come, which was spoken by the mouth of the angel.

Essentially, what Benjamin says is that any time we start thinking too highly of ourselves we would do well to measure our puny selves against our Maker. And when we do that—remembering that this magnificent Being and his magnificent Son care about us, unworthy creatures that we are, and love us, want to remit our sins, want us to rejoin them—we do indeed have cause for humility and great joy.

At this point, Benjamin's tone changes a bit as he begins to describe the life of persons who have chosen to be humble, who have arrived at a new sense of what their Redeemer is destined and willing to do for them, who have turned fully and daily to the Lord in the exercise of great faith. These, Benjamin says, "shall always rejoice, and be filled with the love of God" (with charity), retaining always "a remission of your sins" (4:12). He moves then to something resembling a descriptive code of behavior for his spiritually enlivened, recommitted, repentant people. The remainder of chapter 4 is given to that code. Taken together, Benjamin's injunctions describe the life of a person of charity:

> Ye will not have a mind to injure one another, but to live

peaceably, and to render to every man according to that which is his due.

...ye will not suffer your children that they go hungry, or naked; neither will ye suffer that they transgress the laws of God, and fight and quarrel with one another....

...ye will teach them to love one another, and to serve one another. (4:13–15)

And also, ye yourselves will succor those that stand in need of your succor; ye will administer of your substance unto him that standeth in need; and ye will not suffer that the beggar putteth up his petition to you in vain, and turn him out to perish. (4:16)

Taking the last statement above as a primary text, Benjamin counsels and soundly warns his people against judging the poor to be unworthy of their charity, on the assumption that their "punishments are just" (4:17). Benjamin reminds his listeners that, in fact, we are "all beggars" at the hands of God, totally dependent on him "for all the substance which we have"—food, clothing, and riches "of every kind" (4:19). And now, as you have begged him to forgive your sins, Benjamin asks, have you "begged in vain?" He answers for them: "Nay; he has poured out his Spirit upon you, and has caused that your hearts should be filled with joy" (4:20). Nor does Benjamin stop there. Lest any should forget their debt to their Maker, and their obligation to their fellow beings, he clarifies the matter:

And now, if God, who has created you, on whom you are dependent for your lives and for all that ye have and are, doth grant unto you whatsoever ye ask that is right, in faith, believing that ye shall receive, O then, how ye ought to impart of the substance that ye have one to another. (4:21)

Furthermore, he says, if you should judge and condemn the person who petitions you for help, "how much more just will be your condemnation for withholding your substance, which doth not belong to you but to God, to whom also your life belongeth" (4:22).

As for the poor who are unable to give, what is important is that in their hearts they know that they would give if they could (4:24). Benjamin sums up his plea by informing his people that they will retain a remission of their sins only as they give of their "substance to the poor, every man according to that which he hath, such as feeding the hungry, clothing the naked, visiting the sick and administering to their relief, both spiritually and temporally, according to their wants" (4:26).

Pause with me on those last phrases. As Benjamin defines charity, it involves *spiritual* as well as temporal assistance. In some ways, it is easier to make a monetary contribution, or perform a labor, than it is to "administer" spiritual relief. I suspect that spiritual relief can only be given out of genuine love. I also suspect that what constitutes spiritual need and spiritual relief differs from person to person and requires insightful discernment. We are left with the question: Is charity truly charity unless it is a genuine expression of "pure love"? On the other hand, we should not confuse the modern use of the term "wants" (desires) with Benjamin's use of the term to designate "lacks," or missing essentials.

I confess, however, to being very grateful for Benjamin's added cautionary note that "all these things" are to be "done in wisdom and order; for it is not requisite that a man should run faster than he has strength" (4:27). He recognizes that mortals do have limits to their capabilities.

We sense that Benjamin, if he had the strength, would like to go on and warn his people further against a whole raft of sins (see 4:29), but there are too many to number. He settles for a general, all-inclusive, no-nonsense summation. I picture his audience squirming as he declares:

> But this much I can tell you, that if ye do not watch yourselves, and your thoughts, and your words, and your deeds, and observe the commandments of God, and continue in the faith of what ye have heard concerning the coming of our Lord, even unto the end of your lives, ye must perish. (4:30)

Significantly, the one sin Benjamin chooses for lengthy and pointed counsel in this his final address to his people, before handing the throne to his son, is the lack of charity. We should not underestimate the importance of this choice.

Having concluded his address, Benjamin now desires to know if his people have believed the words he has declared to them. Even though he has spoken from a tower, his audience is so vast that his words had to be copied and distributed to those beyond hearing. He sends among his people yet again, this time asking if they have believed what he has said. We witness their repentance and the joyous remission of their sins in chapter 4, and now their celebratory response affirms that they are "willing to enter into a covenant" of obedience to whatever God commands of them (Mosiah 5:5). Most assuredly it is a covenant of consecration.

This is indeed one of the crests in the Book of Mormon, when an entire people turn from self-centered complacency and sin to unwavering faith and charity. Hear their jubilant cry:

> And they all cried with one voice, saying: Yea, we believe all the words which thou hast spoken unto us; and also, we know of their surety and truth, because of the Spirit of the Lord Omnipotent, which has wrought a mighty change in us, or in our hearts, that we have no more disposition to do evil, but to do good continually. (5:2)

The great change of heart. We will see hearts changed repeatedly throughout the Book of Mormon, assuring us that this miracle is possible in every life. Sometimes it happens gradually, sometimes it happens in a burst of light and joy, after repentance takes us to our knees and the love of God reaches the very depths of our souls. It requires that we see ourselves honestly, that we face what we have been and where we fall short. It requires that we want to change, more than we want anything, even life. It requires that we gladly surrender our wills to his will. It requires an ultimate kind of humility, what Jesus meant when he described himself as meek and lowly of heart. It requires that we love and serve each other. It requires that we become persons who exemplify the pure love of Christ, persons of charity.

So completely do Benjamin's people sense "the infinite goodness of God, and the manifestations of his Spirit," that they "have great views of that which is to come," even believing that, "were it expedient," they "could prophesy of all things" (5:3). They affirm in great joy that it is their faith in the things Benjamin has taught that has brought them "to this great knowledge" (5:4).

Benjamin then explains what the change they have experienced and the covenant they have made mean. They will now "be called the children of Christ, his sons, and his daughters," because "this day he hath spiritually begotten you; . . . your hearts are changed through faith on his name; therefore, ye are born of him and become his sons and his daughters" (5:7). Having become Christ's spiritual offspring, these converted souls now must take upon them his name. (This seems to me something of a parallel with mortal children who bear the name of their earthly fathers.) When the names are recorded of all who covenanted with God that day, it is seen that every soul present, with the exception of little children, had so covenanted and "taken upon" himself or herself the name of Christ (Mosiah 6:2).

So ends the account of that blessed event, and so ends the reign of a remarkable king. His words are not soon forgotten but are rehearsed by a later emissary to a group that had split off from the main Nephite community (see Mosiah 8:3, where the first Ammon teaches Limhi's people). Nearly a century after Benjamin's address, Helaman, grandson of the second Alma, reminds his sons Nephi and Lehi of the teachings of king Benjamin (see Helaman 5:9). Surely, too, Benjamin's teachings were repeated in many a Nephite home and congregation, and I think we can safely assume that those whose hearts were changed and who entered into a covenant with their Lord remained faithful until the end of their days. Yet "many of the rising generation" who were "little children at the time he spake unto his people" and "could not understand" his words fell away and "did not believe the tradition of their fathers" (Mosiah 26:1). As the record says, "their hearts were hardened," and they would neither be baptized nor "join the church" (Mosiah 26:3–4). Unfortunately, as "dissensions" grew "among the brethren," unbelievers "became more numerous" (26:5). Enter pride; exit charity.

But whatever happened later, those people in that magical moment had their hearts changed through the Atonement of Christ as they listened to the words of an angel, words delivered by a righteous ruler at the close of his rule—words bearing witness of the coming Christ, their Redeemer. And I have no doubt that the additional admonition of their noble mortal ruler, to exercise charity until the end of their days, had a part in their lasting conversion. No better way could Benjamin have ended his kingly service.

III

THE TWO ALMAS

The story of the two Almas, father and son, has a seemingly inauspicious beginning at a lovely secluded spot called the waters of Mormon. The importance of this small beginning cannot be overstated, for at these waters a regeneration of faith was to begin that would ultimately spread among both Nephites and Lamanites. The record presents that story twice—first as it happened with Alma, the father, and then later, as it is remembered and taught by his repentant, reborn son. That son, also named Alma, would go on to become one of the greatest prophet-teachers in Nephite history.

But the real beginning of the two Almas' story is earlier still. It is in the record of Zeniff (see Mosiah 9–22) that we read of the lovely moment of grace that occurred at the waters of Mormon and its immediate surrounds. There a group of people once caught under the influence of a corrupt king Noah repent and come together with the first Alma in perfect harmony and love. Events leading up to that moment, however, are not so lovely. Below is a brief summary.

Zeniff, as he says, "being over-zealous to inherit the land of our fathers" (Mosiah 9:3), led a group of his countrymen from Zarahemla to lands the Nephites had once inhabited, lands now occupied by Lamanites. After a number of years, the uneasy truce between the two groups fails, and the Lamanite armies arrive. Fighting "in the strength of the Lord" (9:17), Zeniff's people are victorious. I mention these things because Zeniff, whom Mormon elects to quote directly at first, makes it plain that this generation of Lamanites have had hatred toward Nephites bred into them. They have inherited the conviction that their predecessors were wronged in countless ways (see Mosiah 10:12–16). Having been thus taught that they should "hate" and "murder" and "rob and plunder" the Nephites, "they have an eternal hatred towards" them (Mosiah 10:17).

The principal Lamanite weakness of character, therefore, is quite different from the principal Nephite weakness. The Nephite weakness becomes apparent when Noah succeeds his father Zeniff to the throne and begins to rule over this group of expatriates. Apparently one of Noah's first official acts is to "put down all the priests that had been consecrated by his father" and replace them with "such as were lifted up in the pride of their hearts" (Mosiah 11:5). In other words, he appoints people as faithless and uncharitable as himself to attend him. Pride opens the door to a multitude of other sins, but pride itself tops the list. Luck (not God) is with Noah's people in a subsequent battle with Lamanites, and they take full credit for the victory. They are "lifted up in the pride of their hearts; they did boast in their own strength, saying that their fifty could stand against thousands of the Lamanites; and thus they did boast, and did delight in blood, and the shedding of the blood of their brethren" (11:19).[1] And so, within a few years pride and all its trappings dominate a group of the Lord's chosen people.

Among Noah's subjects, however, is a prophet named Abinadi, and he begins to make a nuisance of himself by crying repentance. With eyes that are "blinded" and hearts that are "hardened" (11:29), the people want him disposed of. A noisy conscience can be terribly bothersome. After two years, presumably spent in hiding, or at least in low profile, a disguised Abinadi returns to teach yet again. Clearly a threat to Noah and his cohorts, Abinadi is brought to court to answer for his insurrection. It appears that Mormon inserted the whole of Abinadi's discourse, both his doctrinal instructions and his bold prophetic warnings, into the record.

Abinadi does not specifically teach the doctrine of charity, but it is implicitly present in this section of the record, in Abinadi's fearless condemnation of mortals who, like Noah and his priests, have "gone according to their own carnal wills and desires; having never called upon the Lord." He extended "the arms of mercy" toward them, but "they would not" heed him, nor would they "depart" from their

---

1. We remember that Captain Moroni was a military leader who did everything in his power to avoid bloodshed (see Alma 48:11 and 55:19), winning many victories through stratagem alone.

iniquities or "repent." Three times Abinadi employs the phrase "they would not" (Mosiah 16:12), emphatically describing the stubbornness and disregard of God that obviously permeates this society as well.

Abinadi's testimony and warning touch the heart of one courageous man, a priest of Noah and a descendant of Nephi. His name is Alma. Abinadi will pay for his testimony with his life, but thanks to Alma, Abinadi's words trigger a renaissance of faith and charity among a small group of people. After bravely pleading Abinadi's case before Noah, Alma is forced to flee for his own life. "Being concealed for many days," and most certainly under the guidance of the Spirit, Alma writes "all the words which Abinadi had spoken" (Mosiah 17:4). And then he begins teaching those words "privately among the people" (Mosiah 18:1). The words quicken the memories of some and take hold in their minds and hearts. What follows is one of the sweetest experiences described in the entire Book of Mormon. A small group that swells to "about four hundred and fifty souls" (18:35) gathers and worships in the bonds of pure love.

Their place of gathering is the waters of Mormon, a sequestered area "in the borders of the land" (18:4), away from the eyes of the king and his minions. Those who believe Alma's teachings come to join him where he hides by "a fountain of pure water" (18:5). There he teaches them "repentance, and redemption, and faith on the Lord" (18:7). They gladly accept baptism "as a witness" of their "covenant with [God]" to "serve him and keep his commandments" (18:10). An important part of their promise is a covenant of charity. These repentant and newly converted saints are, as Alma says, "desirous to come into the fold of God, and to be called his people," and they

> . . . are willing to bear one another's burdens, that they may be light;
>
> Yea, and are willing to mourn with those that mourn; yea, and comfort those that stand in need of comfort, and to stand as witnesses of God at all times and in all things, and in all places. . . . (18:8–9)

These dear souls, "about two hundred and four" (18:16) at this time, "clapped their hands for joy" (18:11) and entered the waters of baptism. Alma and Helam are first, "and they arose and came forth out of the water rejoicing, being filled with the Spirit" (18:14). They then baptize the others "in the waters of Mormon, and [those baptized] were filled with the grace of God. And they were called the church of God, or the church of Christ, from that time forward" (18:16–17). What Alma stresses among members of the newly organized church, in addition to repentance and faith, and the words of the prophets, is charity—pure love. I am deeply moved by the nature of his "commandments" to these spiritually hungry souls. His emphasis is clear as he describes what is expected of mortals who willingly enter into a covenant with their God. It is a description of what the Lord's church should be in any era, including ours. Maybe especially ours because we are blessed with the restored gospel of Jesus Christ in its entirety. The Lord's true church is to be a church in which love and unity abound:

> And he commanded them that there should be no contention one with another, but that they should look forward with one eye, having one faith and one baptism, having their hearts knit together in unity and in love one towards another.
> And thus he commanded them to preach. And thus they became the children of God. (18:21–22)

I love that passage, especially the last sentence. "And thus they became the children of God." That's how it is done, through loving God and loving one another. The two great commandments on which all others hang, the recipe for perfect harmony—unfailing charity.

These saints gather weekly for learning and worship, and whenever else they can. Alma insists on equality among them, the kind of charity that involves sharing one's worldly goods as well as one's spiritual strengths and resources:

> And again Alma commanded that the people of the church should impart of their substance, every one according to that which he had; if he have more abundantly he should impart more abundantly; and of him that had but little, but little should be required; and to him that had not should be given.
> And thus they should impart of their substance of their own free will and good desires towards God, and to those priests that stood in need, yea, and to every needy, naked soul.
> And this he said unto them, *having been commanded of God*; and they did walk uprightly before God, imparting to one another both temporally and spiritually according to their needs and their wants. (18:27–29, emphasis added)

It is clear from the emphasized statement above that the Lord is communicating with Alma, his chosen mouthpiece. This supreme moment of pure love, enhanced by a beautiful natural setting, seems almost out of space, out of time. Too predictably, perhaps, the moment is eventually interrupted by the approach of king Noah's army. The Lord warns these blessed people (see Mosiah 23:1), who now number about 450, of their danger; and they depart into the wilderness with their families. But the summary verse of what happened among them in the area called Mormon captures the experience in poetry, and I simply must quote it:

> And now it came to pass that all this was done in Mormon, yea, by the waters of Mormon, in the forest that was near the waters of Mormon; yea, the place of Mormon, the waters of Mormon, the forest of Mormon, how beautiful are they to the eyes of them who there came to the knowledge of their Redeemer; yea, and how blessed are they, for they shall sing to his praise forever. (Mosiah 18:30)

Notice how skillfully the repetition is done here. In your reading of this passage, break at the first semicolon and observe that the three opening geographical references are repeated in condensed parallel form: "the place of Mormon, the waters of Mormon, the forest of Mormon." All bear the name Mormon—the place, the fountain of water, and the forest. This passage could have been shortened by the record keeper, but he chose to relish the phrases, thus prolonging the beauty of that incredible moment on our tongues as well as in our memories. And perhaps in his. Surely, the man Mormon was moved by the reverence accorded his namesake area centuries before he was born.

Indeed, what occurred at the waters of Mormon was a watershed moment in Nephite history. Its effect was more far-reaching than Alma could have anticipated when he began teaching the words of Abinadi and the Lord to the few humble souls who gathered there. Not only does Mormon give a full account in Mosiah 18, but he inserts two chapters (Mosiah 23 and 24) abridged from Alma's own record of these people. There Alma describes the loving, faithful, nourishing community established and maintained at Helam after his people fled Noah's armies. He had taught them "that every man should love his neighbor as himself, that there should be no contention among them," and the priests who "did watch over" these saints were "consecrated . . . just men" (Mosiah 23:15, 17–18).

Even when this community of believers was discovered and brought into Lamanite bondage, with one of Noah's former turncoat priests in authority over them, they remained faithful through heavy persecution. Forbidden to pray aloud under sentence of death, they "did pour out their hearts" silently to God. He eased their burdens, making them "light," and "they did submit cheerfully and with patience to all the will of the Lord" (Mosiah 24:11–15). And then, having proven themselves in "faith" and "patience" (24:16), these humble servants of God and of each other are delivered by the Lord's hand. They find their way to Zarahemla where king Mosiah welcomes them "with joy" (24:25).

I don't think I have, in the past, fully appreciated the first Alma as the sublimely inspiring, exceptional leader he was. This incredible man was actually baptized by the power of God and given authority directly from God at the waters of Mormon. With that authority, he baptized others and founded the church that became the parent organization in Zarahemla after he and his people arrived there some years later. Once the church was established, king Mosiah appointed him to lead it. We focus attention so much on the miraculous conversion and subsequent ministry of Alma's son, the younger Alma, that we (myself included— once but no longer!) tend to look past the older of these two blessed and blessing prophets and teachers.

❧

So meek and humble was this first Alma ("I am unworthy to glory of myself," Mosiah 23:11) that he had refused to be king of his little community of worshipers, reminding them that the Lord had forbidden that they "esteem one flesh above another, or [that] one man . . . think himself above another," a real danger if kings are not "just men" (23:7–8). Alma has his own personal heartache, however. His son, who bears his name, is not the humble servant of the Lord that his father is—at least not in the beginning. But he was there, with the saints, when they were delivered from bondage and joined Mosiah's people (see Alma 5:5). And it is in Zarahemla that the younger man is at length converted and awakened to a remembrance of his father's teachings, at the waters of Mormon and elsewhere. We know this because he repeatedly refers to those experiences in his own teachings later, as a missionary and father, and as the leader of the church. His was a true, complete conversion, and it *lasted*. He never forgot it, not for a minute.

The second Alma's story really begins with his conversion and the simultaneous conversions of the sons of Mosiah: Aaron, Ammon, Omner, and Himni. And just as these stunning transformations can be traced back to the conversion and teachings of Alma's father, so do the younger men themselves become great watersheds of faith, pure love, and miracles. They are instrumental in the sweeping conversions, heretofore undreamed of, among the Lamanite peoples. These events will be treated in subsequent chapters, but first, I think it important to consider how Alma and his rebellious companions were spending their time before their conversions, to remember what they were doing and saying. Charity was hardly their concern. No one could accuse them of humility or of loving God and their neighbors. No matter that king Mosiah had issued decrees in keeping with the teachings of the church, that "there should be an equality among all men; That they should let no pride nor haughtiness disturb their peace; that every man should esteem his neighbor as himself" (Mosiah 27:3–4).

We are shocked to learn that the sons of Mosiah—who were grandsons of king Benjamin—and the younger Alma, all coming from stalwart parentage, "were numbered among the unbelievers." Not only did this Alma become "a very wicked and an idolatrous man" (27:8), but he was "secretly with the sons of Mosiah seeking to destroy the church" (27:10). We would have expected these particular men, of all people, to be firm in the faith. But just as faithful parents today sometimes see their children reject their teachings and fall away, or even become enemies to the Church, so did the elder Alma and king Mosiah see rebellion in their families. In fact, Mosiah watched not one, but four, sons take that path. I can only imagine the anguish of such parents, then and now.

It is especially hard to picture young Alma, the man we have come to know as a valiant and selfless prophet, in the role of prideful rebel; but this "man of many words" once spent his days flattering the people and leading many to follow his example in iniquity. As we might expect, with his persuasive personal gifts, "he became a great hinderment" to the church, "stealing away the hearts of the people; causing much dissension among the people; giving a chance for the enemy of God to exercise his power over them." There they were,

Alma and the king's sons, sneaking around in secret, doing the devil's work, trying "to destroy the church, and to lead astray the people of the Lord" (27:8–10).

In fact, it takes "an angel of the Lord," speaking "with a voice of thunder" that shakes the earth (27:11), to stop these men in their tracks—literally.[2] All of them fall to the ground, but it is Alma whom the angel addresses specifically, telling him to arise and commanding him in no uncertain terms to "seek to destroy the church no more . . . even if thou wilt of thyself be cast off" (27:16). Needless to say, these rebels are convinced. Overcome with "astonishment," Alma is struck "dumb, that he could not open his mouth" (27:19). Physically helpless, he is carried to his father, who rejoices that the Lord has intervened to rescue his son. The elder Alma and the priests of the church assemble, fasting and praying "for two days and two nights" (27:23) for the younger man's restoration.[3]

Young Alma's strength returns at last and he stands, testifying joyously of his repentance and redemption. "I have repented of my sins," he cries, "and have been redeemed of the Lord; behold, I am born of the Spirit." What a moment this is as Alma experiences, in all its power and glory, the grace of God. He begins immediately to teach what the Lord has told him, "that all mankind . . . must be born again; yea, born of God, changed from their carnal and fallen state, to a state of righteousness" (27:24–25). Most certainly, the spiritual rebirth ("I am born of God," he says again in verse 28) of this once rebellious son is one of the great turning points in the Book of Mormon. It charts a course not only for his people, but also for us.

In fact, the story of the younger Alma's conversion, with Mosiah's sons—expanded quite significantly—becomes an object lesson for Alma when he is teaching his own sons and others as well in future

---

2. This angel, incidentally, is the same fellow who would later send the missionary Alma trekking back to Ammonihah, from whence he had been summarily driven out.

3. Some years later, in Alma's account of this event to his son Helaman, he says that "it was for the space of three days and three nights that I could not open my mouth, neither had I the use of my limbs" (Alma 36:10). He also tells his son Shiblon that he "was three days and three nights in the most bitter pain and anguish of soul" (Alma 38:8).

chapters of the record.[4] Decades later he remembers the details of it vividly. As he rehearses the event to his son Helaman, we learn that his mind was very active during the period when his body was inert (see Alma 36:11ff). Alma describes his suffering in detail, revealing that while he was in a semi-conscious state he remembered all his "sins and iniquities," and "so great" had they been "that the very thought of coming into the presence of my God did rack my soul with inexpressible horror" (36:13–14). In fact, Alma wished that he "could be banished and become extinct both soul and body, that I might not be brought to stand in the presence of my God, to be judged of my deeds" (36:15).

During that time, he remembered only too well his "many sins." But he also remembered hearing his "father prophesy unto the people concerning the coming of one Jesus Christ, a Son of God, to atone for the sins of the world" (36:17). That was the critical moment, the realization of the immense gift of pure love from God, that led him to address his Lord and humbly beseech forgiveness. That was the moment that propelled him into a life of serving others and teaching the true gospel. I have said it before, and I say it again now: We should not forget that the pure love mortals extend to their fellow beings, the charity they feel and live, has its origin with the Father and his Son in the heavens.

I quote a good many of Alma's words to Helaman because no paraphrase or summary could do them justice. It was probably the same for Mormon; he had to quote because in matters such as this, abridgement simply would not serve. And I think he wanted us to experience yet again this magnificent moment in Book of Mormon history. He wanted us to hear Alma, older now, still rejoicing in his miraculous spiritual rebirth and still desiring that every living soul might experience such a rebirth. He has given his life to that cause. No wonder Alma tells his faithful sons his story, and no wonder Mormon included this telling of it to Helaman—and would include a more abbreviated

---

4. The converted people of Ammon, for example, seem to recognize that their own repentance and redemption as a people stem from those conversions. And maybe they take heart in the fact that their teachers underwent a huge change, just as they have done (see Alma 27:25-26).

telling to Shiblon (see Alma 38:6–8).[5] Feel the emotion that fills Alma yet again as he describes for Helaman the instant when the thought of Jesus entered his mind while his soul writhed in torment. This is a man who knows his debt to his loving Savior:

> Now, as my mind caught hold upon this thought, I cried within my heart: O Jesus, thou Son of God, have mercy on me, who am in the gall of bitterness, and am encircled about by the everlasting chains of death. (Alma 36:18)

The moment for repentance and hope had arrived. In that moment of submission and earnest pleading, after days of almost indescribable agony, Alma's repentance was accepted. "When I thought this," he tells his son, "I could remember my pains no more; yea, I was harrowed up by the memory of my sins no more." He goes on, "And oh, what joy, and what marvelous light I did behold; yea, my soul was filled with joy as exceeding as was my pain" (36:19–20)! His eyes were opened to a resplendent vision:

> Yea, methought I saw, even as our father Lehi saw, God sitting upon his throne, surrounded with numberless concourses of angels, in the attitude of singing and praising their God; yea, and my soul did long to be there. (36:22; see also 1 Nephi 1:8)

As I mentioned above, while Alma was still in torment, the thought of entering God's presence terrified him (see Alma 36:14). But then, suddenly, he longed to be in the presence of that very God whom he had dreaded to meet. It was a complete reversal. As he says, "I had been born of God" (36:23). And the result of that rebirth? His heart and mind turned to the welfare of others:

> Yea, and from that time even until now, I have labored without ceasing, that I might bring souls unto repentance; that I might bring them to taste of the exceeding joy of which I did taste; that they might also be born of God, and be filled with the Holy Ghost. (36:24)

---

5. It is not surprising that Alma does not retell the story of his wayward youth, and later conversion, to his son Corianton. That son might have been tempted to use his father's youthful rebellion as an excuse for his own sins. Apparently Corianton repents, for he becomes a faithful missionary.

Alma has risen from selfishness, pride, and disregard for the souls of others to a life absorbed in exercising and living the pure love of Christ. He and the sons of Mosiah have become men of true charity.

Turn now, from Alma's later retelling of his conversion experience, back to the inception of a system of judges among the Nephites, with the spiritually reborn Alma being appointed as the first chief judge.[6] As chief judge he sees that "much affliction" has created "much trial with the church." The reason for "much trial"? Nehor has entered the scene, preaching priestcraft and other spurious notions (see Alma 1:2ff). Nehor gets so much attention that "he began to be lifted up in the pride of his heart, and to wear very costly apparel, yea, and even began to establish a church after the manner of his preaching" (Alma 1:6).

Things deteriorate to the point that "there were many who loved the vain things of the world, and they went forth preaching false doctrines; and this they did for the sake of riches and honor" (1:16). Pride and selfishness have taken hold. In this atmosphere, "the hearts of many were hardened," and their names are removed from the church records. "And also many withdrew themselves" from the church (1:24). Despite the death of Nehor, priestcraft spreads, the faithful saints are persecuted, and all too soon agitation for monarchy arises. Nonetheless, those who remain firm in the faith are "steadfast and immovable in keeping the commandments of God, and they bore with patience the persecution which was heaped upon them" (1:25). They hold true to the principles of charity taught at the waters of Mormon by the elder Alma. They do not become prideful like so many of their neighbors.

The priests generously leave "their labor to impart the word of God," and "the people also left their labors to hear the word of God." Charity continues to flourish among the faithful:

> And the priest, not esteeming himself above his hearers, for the preacher was no better than the hearer, neither was the teacher any better than the learner; and thus they were all equal, and they did all labor, every man according to his strength.
>
> And they did impart of their substance, every man according to that which he had, to the poor, and the needy, and the sick, and

---

6. Recall that a system of judges was instituted by Benjamin's son Mosiah when none of Mosiah's sons would accept the crown (see Mosiah 28:10 and Mosiah 29).

the afflicted; and they did not wear costly apparel, yet they were neat and comely. (1:26–27)

As a result, "they began to have continual peace again," and to "be exceedingly rich, having abundance of all things whatsoever they stood in need" (1:28–29).

There is something especially fine and significant about the participants in the miracles at the waters of Mormon, as at the gathering of Benjamin's people. For a time, at least, they and those under their influence break the pattern so often repeated among the Nephite peoples:

> And thus, in their prosperous circumstances, they did not send away any who were naked, or that were hungry, or that were athirst, or that were sick, or that had not been nourished; and they did not set their hearts upon riches; therefore they were liberal to all, both old and young, both bond and free, both male and female, whether out of the church or in the church, having no respect to persons as to those who stood in need. (1:30)

These people are filled with the pure love of Christ. By contrast, "those who did not belong to their church" fall into the old pattern of "envyings and strife" and self-indulgence—"wearing costly apparel; being lifted up in the pride of their own eyes," and engaging in every other kind of wickedness (1:32).

Sadly enough, however, by "the eighth year of the reign of the judges," the ideal of charity wanes, and "the people of the church began to wax proud, because of their exceeding riches, . . . and all manner of precious things, which they had obtained by their industry; and in all these things were they lifted up in the pride of their eyes, for they began to wear very costly apparel" (Alma 4:6). (I find it interesting that the wearing of costly apparel is repeatedly associated with the increase of pride and the decline of charity in these people.) The record goes on to describe the further dwindling of charity as many in a later generation abandon the principles established years earlier by Alma's father at the waters of Mormon. "Pride" arises as hearts become set "upon riches and upon the vain things of the world," while "contentions," "envyings," and "strife" abound (4:8–9).

Alma grieves deeply over this turn of events, over the "great inequality among the people, some lifting themselves up with their pride, despising others, turning their backs upon the needy and the naked and those who were hungry, and those who were athirst, and those who were sick and afflicted" (4:12). At the same time, there are those who lament what is happening around them and remain faithful, "abasing themselves, succoring those who stood in need of their succor, such as imparting their substance to the poor and the needy, feeding the hungry, and suffering all manner of afflictions, for Christ's sake" (4:13). Alma becomes more and more troubled as he sees persecutions "heaped" on these "humble followers of God" (4:15), these people of lasting charity.

"Seeing no way that he might reclaim" those of his people who have fallen into pride, contention, and worldliness "save it were in bearing down in pure testimony against them," Alma abdicates his judgeship and sets forth to "preach the word of God" (4:19).

Alma begins his mission to reclaim his people in the land of Zarahemla. There and throughout Nephite lands, he delivers a major address, one anchored firmly in the doctrines and principles his father taught. In my last reading of it, the power of that address struck me more forcefully than it ever has before. It is simply magnificent, and it attests to the reality and totality of Alma's conversion. His opening words in that address refer at some length to the blessed events that occurred at Mormon, and to his father's role in those events. Again, we should not underestimate the importance of these things in the younger Alma's mind and in the whole history of Book of Mormon peoples.

It is the changing of hearts at the waters of Mormon that he remembers and the pure love of Christ that flourished there. It is that same pure love that he exemplifies and teaches with all the strength of his being. He asks, "were the bands of death broken, and the chains of hell . . . loosed" at that special place? Then he answers in exalted language: "Yea, they were loosed, and their souls did expand, and they did sing redeeming love" (Alma 5:9). This would not have happened, Alma says, if his father had not experienced "a mighty change . . . in his heart" upon hearing the bold words of the prophet Abinadi (5:12). This is what set off the chain of events that led to the establishment of the divinely authorized church at Mormon and its expansion at Zarahemla and elsewhere. This is what led to the younger Alma's angelic rebuke and conversion, and his subsequent desire that people throughout the land, both in the church and out of the church (see

Alma 5:62), experience that same "redeeming love."

A now mature Alma says it again and again. It was through his father's preaching of the word that "a mighty change was . . . wrought" in the hearts of those who gathered at Mormon. "They humbled themselves and put their trust in the true and living God," and "they were faithful until the end" (5:13). They serve as the example when Alma rhetorically asks the current generation if they have experienced "this mighty change in your hearts," if they have "spiritually been born of God," if they have "received his image in [their] countenances" (5:14, 19). And then he asks the critical question: "if ye have experienced a change of heart, and if ye have felt to sing the song of redeeming love, . . . can ye feel so now" (5:26)? He asks them—and by extension, us—to examine their hearts in matters that relate particularly to charity, to the presence and to the exercise of that splendid gift, the pure love of Christ. In this sermon and elsewhere, Alma frequently teaches through questions, tough rhetorical questions his hearers are to ask themselves:

> Could ye say . . . within yourselves, that ye have been sufficiently humble? That your garments have been cleansed and made white through the blood of Christ . . . ?
> . . . are ye stripped of pride?
> . . . is there one among you who is not stripped of envy?
> . . . is there one among you that doth make a mock of his brother, or that heapeth upon him persecutions? (5:27–30)

Alma also pleads with those "that are puffed up in the vain things of the world" to "hearken unto the voice of the good shepherd, to the name by which ye are called" (5:37–38) and come into his fold. Alma tells his listeners, "speak[ing] in the energy of my soul," that he is a spokesman for the Lord, having been "commanded to stand and testify unto this people the things which have been spoken by our fathers" (5:43–44). In fact, to the members of the church he says, "I, Alma, do command you in the language of him who hath commanded me, that ye observe to do the words which I have spoken unto you" (5:61).

Consider Alma's repeated condemnation of pridefulness and ill treatment of others as he raises another series of pointed rhetorical questions. Again, his questions signify the absence of Christ's pure love, the lack of charity among his people. First, Alma asks his hearers if they "can withstand" the things he is teaching, if they can "lay aside these things, and trample the Holy One under your feet" (5:53). His questions are more than questions; they are condemnations:

> Yea, can ye be puffed up in the pride of your hearts; yea, will ye still persist in the wearing of costly apparel and setting your hearts upon the vain things of the world, upon your riches?
>
> Yea, will ye persist in supposing that ye are better one than another: yea, will ye persist in the persecution of your brethren, who humble themselves and do walk after the holy order of God, . . .
>
> Yea, and will you persist in turning your backs upon the poor, and the needy, and in withholding your substance from them? (5:53–55)

I wonder how many times we, too, have to read these things before we take them to heart. And maybe we forget that gossip and exclusion are forms of uncharitableness, and even persecution.

Alma finds happier circumstances in Gideon, where the people "are established again in the way of [God's] righteousness" (Alma 7:4). But he rehearses for them what he found in Zarahemla, saying in part, "I trust that ye are not lifted up in the pride of your hearts; yea, I trust that ye have not set your hearts upon riches and the vain things of the world" (7:6). He reminds them that they "must repent, and be born again"; otherwise, they "cannot inherit the kingdom of heaven" (7:14). They must covenant with God and enter "the waters of baptism" (7:15). They must consecrate themselves to the Lord's will and work. As I have suggested before, the change of heart is a surrender of self to God, the ultimate expression of humility and pure love. Alma's final counsel to the people of Gideon reminds us of the words both Mormon and Moroni would utter as their civilization plunged toward extinction.[1] It also echoes the teachings of Alma's father at the waters of Mormon and thereafter:

> And now I would that ye should be humble, and be submissive and gentle; easy to be entreated; full of patience and long-suffering; being temperate in all things . . .
>
> And see that ye have faith, hope, and charity, and then ye will always abound in good works. (7:23–24)

---

1. At the close of his ministry, before departing from Zarahemla, "never [to be] heard of more" (Alma 45:18), Alma prophesies the destruction that Mormon and Moroni will experience in person (see the whole of Alma 45).

Alma will sound this theme again and again, even in Ammonihah, a city of apostates where he, with Amulek, would subsequently be imprisoned and tortured for their teachings. In a major address there, speaking "from the inmost part of my heart" (Alma 13:27), he urges charity, again in words that echo his father's words at Mormon. He begs these people, most of them haughty antagonists, to "humble yourselves before the Lord," to be "led by the Holy Spirit, becoming humble, meek, submissive, patient, full of love and all long-suffering." And then he adds the summary trio: "Having *faith* on the Lord; having a *hope* that ye shall receive eternal life; having *the love of God* always in your hearts" (13:28–29, emphases added). Some people believe what he says, but the local power brokers respond by imprisoning and torturing Alma and Amulek and forcing them to witness the burning of whole families of believers, along with their scriptural records (see Alma 14:8).

Let's pause for a reminder of just how these two men met and joined forces, and why they were spared additional abuses in the prison at Ammonihah. Both events were wrought by the miraculous operation of divine grace. First, there was the conversion of Amulek, who at the time was a well-to-do, highly respected resident of Ammonihah. On Alma's first attempt to teach in that city, he had been "reviled" and tossed out of town (Alma 8:13). But a no-nonsense angel stopped Alma in his retreat and sent him back to Ammonihah, where that same angel had prepared Amulek to receive him (see Alma 8:15–21). The once hardhearted and rebellious Amulek (by his own description—see Alma 10:5–6) "obeyed the voice of the angel" (Alma 10:8) and took the half-starved Alma into his home. During the time that Alma "tarried many days with Amulek" (Alma 8:27), we can be sure Alma was preparing his benefactor for their mission to teach a people who "did wax more gross in their iniquities" (8:28).

As they go forth "to declare the words of God," the two men are "filled with the Holy Ghost. And they had power given unto them, insomuch that they could not be confined in dungeons" nor be slain, a power they hold in check until driven to extremes (8:30–31). An extreme moment comes in Ammonihah, after they have been bound and imprisoned, mocked and smitten, spit upon and starved. Finally, with "the power of God . . . upon Alma and Amulek, . . . they rose and stood upon their feet." Alma cries out to the Lord for "deliverance. And they broke the cords with which they were bound" (Alma 14:25–26).

The earth shakes, and the prison walls collapse, killing the judge, the lawyers, and the rest of the tormentors. But "Alma and Amulek came forth out of the prison, and they were not hurt," though everyone else there perishes (14:27–28).

Amulek becomes a powerful teacher in his own right, and his teachings reinforce and add to those of Alma. We hear Amulek stressing the theme of charity a few years later when he and Alma are teaching among the poor of the Zoramites, they who have been denied access to places of worship by the haughty, well-heeled in their land. (The Zoramites, a community of dissenters from the true church, are practicing a strange, schismatic, prideful form of religion.) Amulek enjoins his listeners, who are "poor as to things of the world" as well as "poor in heart" (Alma 32:3), to "humble yourselves and continue in prayer" to God (Alma 34:19), regardless of place or circumstance (see Alma 34:17–27). Moreover, he specifically urges his listeners to "let your hearts be full, drawn out in prayer unto him continually for your welfare, and also for the welfare of those who are around you" (34:27). Then he enlarges on the subject and issues a warning:

> Do not suppose that this is all; for after ye have done all these things, if ye turn away the needy, and the naked, and visit not the sick and afflicted, and impart of your substance, if ye have, to those who stand in need—I say unto you, if ye do not any of these things, behold, your prayer is in vain, and availeth you nothing, and ye are as hypocrites who do deny the faith.
>
> Therefore, if ye do not remember to be charitable, ye are as dross which the refiners do cast out (it being of no worth) and is trodden under foot of men. (34:28–29)

Amulek repeatedly counsels these people to "harden not your hearts" (34:31), because "that same spirit which doth possess your bodies at the time that ye go out of this life, that same spirit will have power to possess your body in that eternal world" (34:34). He insists that they "contend no more against the Holy Ghost," but "take upon" themselves "the name of Christ" and

> . . . humble yourselves to the dust, and worship God, in whatsoever place ye may be in, in spirit and in truth; and . . . live in thanksgiving daily, for the many mercies and blessings which he doth bestow upon you. (34:38)

It is charity Amulek continues to emphasize as he concludes his sermon by exhorting these people "to have patience," and to "bear with all manner of afflictions." They are not to "revile against those who do cast you out because of your exceeding poverty, lest ye become sinners like unto them." He says it again, "Have patience, and bear with those afflictions, with a firm hope that ye shall one day rest from all your afflictions" (34:40–41). What a team Alma and Amulek made!

We have seen miracles aplenty, but we are not finished with miracles, for they begin to multiply among the Lamanites. Unlike the majority of prideful, unloving, apostate Nephites, thousands of Lamanites humbly open their hearts to the word of God and to infusions of the Spirit.

IV

LAMANITE CONVERSIONS: LAMONI

When we consider the great events that would follow the conversion of Alma—along with Aaron, Ammon, Omner, and Himni—we realize just how important this single event was. The Lord reached out to one man, and in so doing not only touched his partners in crime, but also introduced the gospel of Jesus Christ to many thousands who were strangers to it. The task of these converted companions was not an easy one, for they would preach "the word of God in much tribulation, being greatly persecuted" and "smitten" by the "unbelievers" (Mosiah 27:32) while "striving to repair all the injuries which they had done to the church" (27:35). Their transformation, through "much anguish of soul" (Mosiah 28:4), from enemies of God and his church to "instruments in the hands of God," teaching and "publish[ing] peace" (27:36–37), was nothing short of miraculous. From men of pride and hate they became, through repentance and the Lord's "infinite mercy" (Mosiah 28:4), men of humility and infinite love. Men of charity.

Having refused the crown and having taught among the Nephites, king Mosiah's sons approach their father and ask permission to travel, with a few select others, "to the land of Nephi" to "impart the word of God to their brethren, the Lamanites." They desire to "bring them to the knowledge of the Lord their God" and possibly "cure them of their hatred towards the Nephites, that they might also be brought to rejoice in the Lord their God," and that contentions would cease "in all the land" (28:1–2). So changed are these men that "they could not bear that any human soul should perish; yea, even the very thoughts that any soul should endure endless torment did cause them to quake and tremble" (28:3). Mosiah, after many days of hearing his sons' entreaties, goes to the Lord for guidance. He is told to "let them go up, for many shall believe on their words, and they shall have eternal life." The Lord also promises that their lives will be spared (28:7).

They journey into the wilderness, lone Nephites setting out for hostile territory, fasting and praying that the Lord's Spirit would be with them, that they might be his instruments in teaching their Lamanite brethren. The Lord sends the comfort of his Spirit and promises that if they are patient in suffering and afflictions, he will indeed "make an instrument of thee in my hands unto the salvation of many souls" (Alma 17:10–11). What is both impressive and frightening to me is that, after receiving blessing and instruction from Ammon, their apparent leader, the brothers and friends separate, each going "forth . . . , every man alone" on "their several journeys throughout the land" (17:13, 17–18). I try to imagine their thoughts as they embarked on their solitary ways, on missions that would last fourteen years, missions on which some of them would be beaten and starved and cast into prisons. But in the end, they would see a nation of godless enemies become a nation of untold numbers of believing, loving, godfearing people. As Moroni would observe centuries later, a great miracle was "wrought" through the faith of these missionaries (Ether 12:15). And unlike many of their fickle Nephite brethren, the spiritually reborn Lamanites would never forsake their newfound faith, nor fail in the pure love of Christ.

Consider now our beloved Ammon, that sweet, gentle (usually!) giant. I love him like a brother. This is a man of infinite humility and charity, a physically powerful man who could well have led armies if he had listened to his uncharitable Nephite countrymen. These countrymen scorned Ammon and his brothers for thinking they could turn a bloodthirsty enemy into peaceful neighbors and fellow-worshipers. The prideful Nephites wanted instead to take up arms and wipe the Lamanites off the map (see Alma 26:23–25). But Ammon and his brothers knew a better way. As Ammon says, "we came into the wilderness not with the intent to destroy our brethren, but with the intent that perhaps we might save some few of their souls" (Alma 26:26).

Even as I write these words, I glance over to a small sign displayed above my desk. It reads, "Peace also takes courage." Indeed it does. And peace is what is wrought among a vast nation of Lamanites whose hearts are opened to the Spirit. Their hearts are changed because a few men, armed not with weapons of war but with faith, hope, and charity, had the courage to teach the gospel of Jesus Christ to them. Men can be subdued by the sword, but their hearts and minds can only be won by the word, especially the word of God, and by love. This is a vital message of the Book of Mormon to our day (see especially Alma 31:5).

Life was by no means easy for these peace-loving missionaries whose only purpose and labor was to teach out of love. For their efforts, Ammon says, "We have been cast out, and mocked, and spit upon, and smote upon our cheeks; and we have been stoned, and taken and bound with strong cords, and cast into prison." He adds, "And we have suffered all manner of afflictions, and all this, that perhaps we might be the means of saving some soul" (Alma 26:29–30). He credits God for their safe deliverance and for their great joy in bringing countless souls to spiritual rebirth and newness of life.

The miracle begins in a simple, unmiraculous way. Ammon is arrested as he enters the land of Ishmael and is taken before the Lamanite king of that area, a man named Lamoni. The king can dispose of Ammon at his "pleasure," either slay him or imprison him or make him a slave (Alma 17:20). But so unassuming and humble is Ammon, and so willing to make his home among the Lamanites, that the king is won over, even offering one of his daughters to Ammon for a wife. Ammon graciously declines, asking instead to be a servant to the king. All readers of the Book of Mormon know the story of Ammon, who serves faithfully, managing to save both the king's flocks and the lives of his servants in the process. And it is this faithful service—even to remembering the king's order to prepare his horses and chariots for a journey, when a lesser man might have paraded about as a hero—that opens the king's heretofore closed mind. In fact, so astonishing are Ammon's deeds that Lamoni and his servants are ready to believe that Ammon is God himself, the "Great Spirit" of Lamanite tradition (17:2).

The conversion of Lamoni, his queen, and his household is one of those splendid moments of grace in the Book of Mormon. Its consequences ripple throughout the larger Lamanite nation, and they are lasting. Only the ambitious Amalekites and Amulonites, apostate Nephites who have joined with the unconverted Lamanites and stirred them to hatred and war, are immune to the teachings of Ammon and his brothers. When Ammon approaches the king to report that the horses and chariot are ready, he can see "that the countenance of the king was changed" (Alma 18:12). The king remains silent.

Something is happening here, and the Spirit enables Ammon to read Lamoni's thoughts. If Ammon were a prideful, power-seeking man, he could make any demand at this moment and the king would accede to it. But what does Ammon say? Not that he is a god, or an angel, or any such thing, but rather, "I am a man, and am thy servant; therefore, whatsoever thou desirest which is right, that will I do" (18:17). Isn't that amazing? Ammon insists, although the king is essentially in his power, that he is only the king's servant and wishes to serve him in things that are right.

The king, sensing something more than human in Ammon, something spiritually beyond his own comprehension, offers to grant Ammon anything he desires. This is the opening Ammon has been waiting for. (I love the passage that describes Ammon as "wise, yet harmless," 18:22. Wise, oh yes, but harmless? To Lamoni, maybe, but not to the plunderers of the king's flocks at the waters of Sebus. Of course, Ammon could have slain them all. But he settled for killing some and cutting off the arms of others—apparently not an unusual practice among some ancient peoples.) Ammon asks only that Lamoni "hearken unto my words" as he tells Lamoni "by what power" he is able to perform superhuman feats (18:22). Lamoni agrees "to believe all [his] words" (18:23), and the teaching begins.

Ammon starts at the beginning with the identity of God, the great Creator. When Lamoni asks Ammon if he is "sent from God," Ammon, not wanting to be mistaken for a heavenly messenger, humbly says, "I am a man; . . . and I am called by his Holy Spirit to teach these things unto this people, that they may be brought to a knowledge of that which is just and true." But he adds, "And a portion of that Spirit dwelleth in me, which giveth me knowledge, and also power according to my faith and desires which are in God" (18:33–35). And so Ammon teaches the Lamanite king and his household of the Creation and the Fall. Then he lays "before him the records and the holy scriptures" (18:36). He also rehearses "the rebellions of Laman and Lemuel, and the sons of Ishmael." Most important, Ammon teaches "the plan of redemption" and "the coming of Christ, and all the works of the Lord" (18:38–39).

Miracle of miracles, "the king believed all his words" (18:40). The king cries out to the Lord for mercy, on himself and on his people. And then he falls to earth, "as if he were dead" (18:41–42). After two days, the queen, reluctant to bury her husband, summons Ammon. Again, he does not assert himself but waits to be called, knowing that she is now ready to hear his words and that Lamoni is not dead but is "under the power of God" (Alma 19:6). This single, individual event becomes the trigger point for the conversion of Lamoni's father, king over all the Lamanites, and the conversion of a huge portion of the Lamanite nation. Perhaps Ammon can't see that ultimate outcome just now, but he knows what is happening inside Lamoni and he rejoices. He knows

> that the dark veil of unbelief was being cast away from [Lamoni's] mind, and the light which did light up his mind, which was the light of the glory of God . . . had infused such joy into his soul . . . that the light of everlasting life was lit up in his soul, yea, he knew that this had overcome his natural frame, and he was carried away in God. . . . (19:6)

Ammon tells the queen that Lamoni is not dead, but "sleepeth in God," and will rise up the next day (19:8). She believes him, though her only witness is his word. He says that her faith far exceeds that of the Nephites.

At the appointed time, Lamoni's household witnesses the blessed moment of divine grace. Lamoni rises, praising God and testifying: "Blessed be the name of God. . . . I have seen my Redeemer; and he shall come forth, and be born of a woman, and he shall redeem all mankind who believe on his name" (19:12–13). Think on that statement for a moment. So willing was Lamoni to believe Ammon's teachings, and so ready to receive the Savior into his heart and mind, that the Savior himself has appeared to this Lamanite king and borne witness of his forthcoming earthly ministry and atoning mission. Such an appearance powerfully demonstrates the Savior's love for this man and his people. It also affirms the huge significance of this one single conversion.

Having spoken these words in a fulness of joy, Lamoni is "overpowered by the Spirit," and he and the queen both sink to the earth (19:13). Ammon, deeply moved with gratitude at the ministrations of the Lord and the Spirit in these former enemies of his people, falls to his knees and "pour[s] out his soul in prayer and thanksgiving to God." Like Lamoni and his queen, he too sinks to earth, "overpowered with joy" (19:14). This is an unforgettable moment.

There is some alarm, however, when a servant woman named Abish, a secret convert of many years, spreads news of this event in the hope that others will see and believe. The townspeople arrive, many of them agitated and assuming the worst. But when Abish touches the queen's hand, the queen arises and takes the king's hand. At her touch, he rises to his feet and begins to teach the words of Ammon, who also stands and with the servants begins to minister. The servants all testify "that their hearts had been changed; that they had no more desire to do evil." They go forth teaching others of God, declaring "unto the people that they had seen angels and had conversed with them" (19:33–34). Picture in your mind the stunning wonder of this event that only a short time ago would have seemed impossible. Angels (plural!) descend and participate in the launching of a new era for these blessed descendants of father Lehi's rebellious sons. Many believe and are baptized. They become righteous and "establish a church" of the faithful (19:35).

Clearly, Mormon is fully aware of the significance of this amazing event as the Lamanite people begin turning to God, and God to them. He says,

> And thus the work of the Lord did commence among the Lamanites; thus the Lord did begin to pour out his Spirit upon them; and we see that his arm is extended to all people who will repent and believe on his name. (19:36)

I can't help contrasting the glad, humble response of this Lamanite pair against the proud king Noah's rejection of Abinadi's teachings and his execution of that brave prophet. The heart of Noah, a Nephite, like the hearts of the people around him, was hard. We will see in Lamoni's father, too, the same humility we saw in his son, an openness to the doctrine of Christ, at whatever cost.

V

LAMANITE CONVERSIONS: LAMONI'S FATHER

It appears that Ammon remains, at least for a time, in the land of Ishmael, the land over which Lamoni is king. Not until "they had established a church in that land" do he and Lamoni head out together (Alma 20:1). Lamoni had persuaded Ammon to accompany him to the land of Nephi, a land occupied by Lamanites for many years, to meet his father, the chief king over all Lamanite lands and peoples. The Lord intervenes, however, warning Ammon that Lamoni's father will try to kill him. Ammon is sent instead to Middoni, to deliver his brother Aaron and other missionaries from prison. Lamoni accompanies him, thinking to persuade his friend, the king of Middoni, to release the prisoners. As luck would have it, they meet Lamoni's father on the road, and he is not happy with his son. Not only did Lamoni miss the big Lamanite festival, but he is now in the company of a Nephite—unforgivable on both counts.

When Lamoni explains what had detained him and where he is going, his angry father commands Lamoni to kill Ammon. Lamoni refuses, a bold and dangerous thing to do. The irate father reflexively raises his sword against his son, and Ammon intervenes, defending Lamoni against his father. The great king then turns his attack to Ammon, who rather handily renders him weaponless and helpless. Now fearing for his life, the king pleads with Ammon, saying, "If thou wilt spare me I will grant unto thee whatsoever thou wilt ask, even to half of the kingdom" (Alma 20:23). Ammon is not interested in worldly power or position. All he asks is the release of his brethren from prison and the right for Lamoni to retain his kingdom and to run it according to his own will and desire. When the king sees that "Ammon had no desire to destroy him," and that Ammon has "great love . . . for his son Lamoni," the astonished magistrate grants all that Ammon asks (20:26). As I have said, if the pen is mightier than the sword, surely love is mightier still.

What the older man has seen and heard reaches into his once-implacable soul. Ammon's great charity, his pure love, and Lamoni's words make this great king hunger for what they know. This seemingly inauspicious incident, though important to the three persons involved, would open the door for huge turning of hearts in the larger Lamanite kingdom. Although it is Aaron who eventually teaches the great king, the heart of that king would not have been softened toward the word of God if it had not been touched by Ammon's words, and by his example of honor and charity.

Let us go now to the account of Aaron, after he has been released from serving time in prison for teaching among the Amalekites and Amulonites. Although Nephites by blood, these ambitious apostates have become Lamanites geographically and politically.[1] And they have further poisoned minds and hardened hearts among their adoptive allies. But with the arrival in Middoni of Ammon and Lamoni, and the release of "Aaron and a certain number of his brethren" (Alma 21:13–14), the Lamanite people begin to listen and many come "to the knowledge of the truth" (21:17). Ammon and Lamoni then return to teach again in the land of Ishmael, Lamoni's home, where Lamoni institutes religious freedom among his people. Lamoni teaches them, as does Ammon, and they are converted in great numbers.

Meanwhile Aaron is "led by the Spirit to the land of Nephi, even to the house of the king [Lamoni's father] which was over all the land save it were the land of Ishmael" (Alma 22:1). (Ishmael is the land over which he had given Lamoni total jurisdiction.) Aaron approaches this mighty king in the same humble manner as Ammon had approached Lamoni. After introducing himself and his companions as "brethren of Ammon," he says, "O king, if thou wilt spare our lives, we will be thy servants" (22:2–3). The king, however, is already a changed man, a man "troubled in mind because of the generosity and the greatness of

---

1. More and more, the term "Lamanite" has come to designate not ethnicity, but rejection of Nephite leadership and religion.

the words of [their] brother Ammon" (22:3). Note that it is the *generosity* of Ammon, as well as the greatness of the words he speaks, that has reached into the soul of this mighty and once-tyrannical king. He has apparently been looking for Ammon to come and teach him.

So open are his mind and heart to the words of life that when Aaron says Ammon has been called to teach elsewhere by "the Spirit of the Lord," the king picks up on the phrase. He wants to know about that Spirit, saying, "this is the thing which doth trouble me" (22:4–5). And he also wants to know what Ammon meant by saying that if the king would repent, he would be saved, but if he would not repent he would "be cast off at the last day" (22:6). The great monarch over all the Lamanite lands is eager to hear the words of salvation. Unlike the poor among the Zoramites whom the younger Alma teaches, a people compelled to be humble because of their afflictions (see Alma 32), this man has untold wealth and power. He *chooses* to humble himself and be taught, and by a traditional enemy at that. As Alma would teach the Zoramites, "blessed are they who humble themselves without being compelled to be humble" (Alma 32:16).

Think back. If the first Alma had not heard Abinadi testify, if he had not begun to teach Abinadi's words and to draw people to the waters of Mormon, if he had not had a son named Alma and prayed for his repentance and redemption, if that son had not been visited and rebuked by an angel in the presence of Ammon and Aaron and two of their brothers, and if Ammon had not found favor with Lamoni and touched his heart with the message of Christ, very likely Aaron would not be poised at this moment to teach the saving gospel to Lamoni's father—the head Lamanite king. This is the moment from which would virtually explode the greatest surge of newfound faith, prior to the arrival of Christ himself, in Book of Mormon history.

And so Aaron begins to teach, again starting with the basics, asking the king if he believes that there is a God. The king knows that the Amalekites say there is a God, and that his own tradition tells of a Great Spirit. So ready is he to believe Aaron's words that he says, "And if now thou sayest there is a God, behold I will believe" (Alma 22:7). He says it again: "Tell me concerning all these things, and I will believe thy words" (22:11). Try to imagine the magnitude and miracle of what we are witnessing, and what must have been going through Aaron's mind. He has come from torture and prison to the throne of a mighty and once-prideful king who begs a humble missionary to teach him the things of eternity.

And teach him Aaron does, beginning as always with the Creation and the Fall. Reading from scripture, he lays out "the plan of redemption . . . through Christ, for all whosoever would believe on his name" (22:13). It is for fallen man, Aaron says, that Christ suffered and died, to "atone for their sins, through [their] faith and repentance." Through him, Aaron continues, "the grave shall have no victory, and . . . the sting of death should be swallowed up in the hopes of glory" (22:14). The king feels the truth of these words in his very soul, and he cries out:

> What shall I do that I may have this eternal life of which thou hast spoken? Yea, what shall I do that I may be born of God, having this wicked spirit rooted out of my breast, and receive his Spirit, that I may be filled with joy, that I may not be cast off at the last day?

And then comes this amazing offer, which is almost incomprehensible to us, so accustomed are we to the ambitions and greed of worldly mortals:

> Behold, said he, I will give up all that I possess, yea, I will forsake my kingdom, that I may receive this great joy. (22:15)

Read that statement again. It is the measure of the man, and the measure of his spiritual readiness. He would gladly surrender his great kingdom and vast possessions in exchange for the saving gospel of Jesus Christ. Everything.

Aaron promises the king that if he will "bow down before God," repenting of all his sins, calling on the Lord's "name in faith, believing that ye shall receive," then indeed his hope will be realized (22:16). I can scarcely read these next words without weeping, and without thinking of the Prophet Joseph's simple, humble prayer in the grove many centuries later, a prayer that would lead to the translation of this sweet utterance. My heart is full at this moment as I cast myself back in time and witness the great king

> . . . bow down before the Lord, upon his knees; yea, even he did prostrate himself upon the earth, and cried mightily saying:
> O God, Aaron hath told me that there is a God; and if there is a God, and if thou art God, wilt thou make thyself known unto me, and I will give away all my sins to know thee, and that I may be raised from the dead, and be saved at the last day. (22:17–18).

And I will give away all my sins to know thee. Ponder that statement. There is a lesson for a lifetime in that one sincere expression of sacrifice, which is perhaps a greater sacrifice even than kingdoms and possessions. It may well be the key to knowing him, our Lord, and ultimately the key to living in his presence eternally. And from whom do we learn this simple lesson? From the most powerful man in the Lamanite nation, a man who has been without God all his life, a man who has now gone humbly to his knees before his Maker, a man who has come to know and express the pure love of Christ.

Having spoken these words, the king—like the younger Alma on his conversion, and Lamoni on his—is "struck as if he were dead" (22:18). We can readily imagine the stir such an event would cause, not only in the king's household, but also among his people. Realizing the danger when the queen arrives and sounds the alarm, Aaron extends his hand and raises the king to his feet. Immediately, that powerful magistrate begins to teach, converting his entire household to the Lord. The Spirit emanates from him with indescribable power, rolling forth through his household and then through his kingdom.

Again, the conversion of just one man, and his national proclamation of religious freedom, gives Aaron and his fellow missionaries access to homes, temples, and sanctuaries throughout the land. Churches are established, priests and teachers are consecrated, "and thousands were brought to the knowledge of the Lord" and "to believe in the traditions of the Nephites" (Alma 23:5). And the incredible thing, the thing that so distinguishes the converted Lamanites from the inconstant Nephites, is that "as many of the Lamanites as believed" in the preaching of Ammon, Aaron, and their fellow missionaries, "and were converted unto the Lord, *never did fall away*" (23:6, emphasis added). And as we shall see, their vows would all too soon be put to the ultimate test.

VI

LAMANITE CONVERSIONS:
THE PEOPLE OF ANTI-NEPHI-LEHI

Lamanites in city after city, land after land, throughout the kingdom, "become a righteous people; they did lay down the weapons of their rebellion, that they did not fight against God any more, neither against any of their brethren" (Alma 23:7; see also Alma 8–13). Only one Amalekite is converted (see 23:14)—now there is a story I'd love to read—and no Amulonites. No surprise there. The single convert among these hardened apostates is the miracle. As for the converted Lamanites, they change their name, to distinguish them from their brethren who remain under the influence of the apostates. They adopt the name "Anti-Nephi-Lehies," which in translation probably means something like "they of," or "ones of" Nephi and Lehi.[1] These saintly people become industrious and friendly with their former enemies and, significantly, "the curse of God did no more follow them" (23:18). Prior to his death, the great Lamanite king confers the larger kingdom on another son, Lamoni's brother, and gives that son the name Anti-Nephi-Lehi (see Alma 24:3).

These are dangerous times for the former Lamanites who, with changed hearts, are filled with faith and the pure love of Christ. The unconverted Lamanites are inflamed to hatred against their brethren by the Amalekites and Amulonites and are making preparations for

---

1. The entry in the *Book of Mormon Reference Companion*, ed. Dennis L. Largey (Salt Lake City: Deseret Book, 2003), 67, suggests this reading of "Anti," rather than our usual understanding of the word as "against."

war. Council is held among the missionaries and the leaders of the converted to determine a defense strategy. Amazingly, the only defense Anti-Nephi-Lehi will entertain is pacifism, non-defense in the usual sense of the term. The only defense is faith and trust in God, and a rare and beautiful humility.

> Now there was not one soul among all the people who had been converted unto the Lord that would take up arms against their brethren; nay, they would not even make any preparations for war; yea, and also their king commanded them that they should not. (Alma 24:6)

The new king, Anti-Nephi-Lehi, speaks to his people, and his words are full of gratitude to God that he has softened their hearts toward their Nephite brethren, and in his great mercy forgiven them for their evil deeds. The king indicates that out of love, God has sent angels to minister among them. In a highly dramatic and symbolic gesture, the king asks his people to bury their swords, that they may never be stained with the blood of their brethren. "And if," he says, "our brethren destroy us, behold, we shall go to our God and shall be saved" (24:16). And so these once unbelieving, often ferocious, people bury their swords "deep in the earth . . . vouching and covenanting with God, that rather than shed the blood of their brethren they would give up their own lives; and rather than take away from a brother they would give unto him; and rather than spend their days in idleness they would labor abundantly with their hands" (24:17–18). This is the power of love, of charity, and of faith.

Mormon's comment here emphasizes what he had observed earlier: "And thus we see that, when these Lamanites were brought to believe and to know the truth, they were firm, and would suffer even unto death rather than commit sin" (24:19). And that is precisely what happens. When the unconverted in league with the apostates come to destroy these changed people and their king, they neither run nor give battle. Rather, they "went out to meet them, and prostrated themselves before them to the earth, and began to call on the name of the Lord." And true to form, their enemies "fall upon them" and start "to slay them with the sword" (24:21). This scene is almost more than one can bear to envision. A thousand and five of these sweet, repentant, loving people are hewn down without offering any resistance. They willingly "lie down and perish," praising "God even in the very act of perishing under the sword" (24:23). What a lesson for us.

There is both a horror and a beauty in this event. I think to myself, Would I have wanted them to break their vow and defend themselves with swords? I guess I wouldn't, though I anguish over their slaughter and wonder if I would have half their courage. But from their sacrifice comes an unexpected changing of hearts and still more widespread conversion of once recalcitrant Lamanites. Touched by the fearless devotion they are witnessing, many of the warriors' hearts are "swollen in them for those of their brethren who had fallen," and they throw "down their weapons of war, and they would not take them up again." Consequently, "the people of God were joined that day by more than the number who had been slain" (24:24–26). As we might have expected, most of the killing was done by the apostate Amalekites and Amulonites, none of whom was converted. Those whose hearts are changed are "actual descendants of Laman and Lemuel" (24:29).

Mormon says it again as he draws lessons for us from the record: "After a people have been once enlightened by the Spirit of God, . . . and then have fallen away into sin and transgression, they become more hardened, and thus their state becomes worse than though they had never known these things" (24:30). This seems to hold true in our day too. The fiercest and most irresponsible critics of The Church of Jesus Christ of Latter-day Saints today are often those who have left it. Unwilling simply to back away, they seem bent on justifying their choice for disbelief by finding fault with the Church, its leaders, and its people.

The rampages go on, and the martyrdoms continue elsewhere, as do the conversions of other Lamanites who remember the teachings of the missionaries, teachings they had once rejected. All who join with the people of Anti-Nephi-Lehi "bury their weapons of war, . . . as their brethren had, and they [begin] to be a righteous people" (Alma 25:14). That these humble, repentant people never falter is evidenced strongly in a later episode. We have seen in them, and will continue to see, the pure love of Christ as it is lived and expressed throughout a lifetime.

Chapter 26 of the book of Alma is another happy interlude in the Book of Mormon. I smile and smile whenever I read it, and it may well explain why I find Ammon so irresistibly lovable. Nearly the whole chapter is given to his irrepressible exuberance over the incredible success of the Nephite mission to the Lamanites. In this chapter we see more than a glimpse into the nature of this physically indomitable, yet tender and soft-hearted man who is so susceptible to motions of the Spirit that he swoons, not once but twice, in the record (see Alma 19:14, 17 and Alma 27:16). This chapter also shows the contrast between the ebullient Ammon and his more reserved brother, Aaron. Mormon must have delighted in this passage, too, because he apparently inscribes all of Ammon's words.

Ammon is so full of joy that he cannot contain it, and he spills it out to his companions. Over and over he exults at the blessings bestowed not only upon the converted Lamanites, but "upon us," as "instruments in the hands of God to bring about this great work" (Alma 26:3). Waxing poetic, he describes what has happened as a metaphor of the harvest in a ripe field, the sheaves now gathered in and safe from the storms. Dear, dear Ammon, he simply cannot contain his joy and gratitude as he cries out in what can only be described as a song of thanksgiving:

> Blessed be the name of our God; let us sing to his praise, yea, let us give thanks to his holy name, for he doth work righteousness forever. (26:8)

Aaron, the record says, "rebuked" Ammon, saying, "thy joy doth carry thee away unto boasting" (26:10).

Does the large-hearted Ammon take offense or cease his verbal celebration? Not a chance. In fact, Aaron's words trigger a whole new volley of gratitude and elation in his brother. Ammon sings out with even lengthier praise and thanksgiving, insisting that it is in God he boasts, not himself. "Behold," he cries, "my joy is full, yea my heart is brim with joy, and I will rejoice in my God," and "we will praise his name forever" (26:11–12). He goes on and on, through thirty-seven verses, insisting, "I cannot say the smallest part which I feel" (26:16). I certainly credit him for trying, and I notice that Aaron wisely does not try to interrupt his unrestrainable brother again.

I think it significant, too, that as Ammon approaches the conclusion of what has become a combined sermon and prayer—concluded with "Amen" (26:37)—one word is repeated four times. That word is "love," and it is meant in its most expansive applications to the people whose hearts have been changed. Love now fills their lives, as Ammon says, and it is "love towards their brethren and also towards us" (26:31). This love is the motivating factor behind their burying of weapons (26:32) and allowing their brethren to slay them. Surely Ammon is right in exclaiming that never "has there been so great love in all the land . . . even among the Nephites" (26:33). These dear souls, so full of selfless charity, "have gone to their God, because of their love and of their hatred to sin" (26:34). Truly, this is the pure love of Christ, beyond most of our imaginings.

The Lamanite peoples converted at this time never waver in their love, in their dedication to God, or in their vows against violence. Threats come, testing them again, as the frustrated Amalekites and resurgent Lamanites turn their fury once more on the Anti-Nephi-Lehies. And once more these precious saints refuse to take up arms to defend themselves by slaying others, suffering "themselves to be slain according to the desires of their enemies" (Alma 27:3). Ultimately, after Ammon inquires of the Lord, it is decided—and generously agreed to by the Nephites—that the land of Jershon will be given to these people, and that the Nephite armies will protect them. From this time on, they are "called by the Nephites the people of Ammon" (27:26). From then on, they are

> . . . numbered among the people who were of the church of God. And they were also distinguished for their zeal towards God, and also towards men; for they were perfectly honest and upright in all things; and they were firm in the faith of Christ, even unto the end.
>
> And they did look upon shedding the blood of their brethren with the greatest abhorrence; and they never could be prevailed upon to take up arms against their brethren; and they never did look upon death with any degree of terror, for their hope and views of Christ and the resurrection; therefore, death was swallowed up to them by the victory of Christ over it . . .
>
> And thus they were a zealous and beloved people, a highly favored people of the Lord. (27: 27–28, 30)

I stand in awe at that kind of faith and that depth of love.

One measure of their faith and fortitude is their response to the persuasions of the anti-Christ, Korihor, after they are established in the land of Jershon. Korihor has had much success in Zarahemla, where he led "away the hearts of many, causing them to lift up their heads in their wickedness" (Alma 30:18). That old Nephite nemesis, pride, rears its ugly head. Korihor's reception among the people of Ammon is very different. They will have nothing to do with the man. Being "more wise than many of the Nephites," these righteous people "took him, and bound him, and carried him before Ammon, who was a high priest over that people" (30:20). The troublemaker is promptly deported.

There would be still other tests of their faith. The unrepentant Zoramites are infuriated when the people of Ammon welcome the humble, needy converts whom the haughty Zoramites had cast out of Antionum. (They didn't want these people in their neighborhood, but they didn't want anyone else to take them in either. The old "dog in the manger" attitude.) The Zoramite leader sends his henchmen to issue dire threats against the people of Ammon if they do not expel the exiles. But the courageous, peace-loving Anti-Nephi-Lehies do "not fear their words," and do "not cast them out." Rather, they "receive all the poor of the Zoramites that came over unto them; and they did nourish them, and did clothe them, and did give unto them lands for their inheritance; and they did administer unto them according to their wants" (Alma 35:8–9). These blessed people are the very essence of charity, the pure love of Christ. The change in them, as I have said, is permanent.

Wars rage again, and the Nephites, whose military leaders are Captain Moroni and such officers as the second Alma's son, Helaman, are endangered by enemies without and dissenters within. Seeing these perilous circumstances, the people of Ammon are "moved with compassion" and unwilling that their Nephite protectors should die in their defense. The people of Ammon prepare to "take up arms in the defence [sic] of their country" despite their vow, but Helaman and other Nephite leaders convince them not "to break the oath which they had made," fearing "lest by so doing they should lose their souls" (Alma 53:13–14). But there is another way for them to help: "they had many sons, who had not entered into a covenant that they would not take their weapons of war to defend themselves against their enemies" (53:16).

VII

LAMANITE CONVERSIONS:
THE STRIPLING WARRIORS

Another measure of the stalwart constancy of the Lamanite converts is the upright faith and courage of their young sons, and presumably their daughters too. These fine sons, who "called themselves Nephites" (Alma 53:16), also enter into a covenant, but one quite different from that of their parents. Two thousand of them "covenant to fight for the liberty of the Nephites, yea, to protect the land unto the laying down of their lives," vowing "that they never would give up their liberty, but they would fight . . . to protect the Nephites and themselves from bondage." And so, they who "never had hitherto been a disadvantage to the Nephites," have now become "also a great support; for they took their weapons of war, and they would that Helaman should be their leader." These young men were not only "exceedingly valiant for courage," but they were also "men who were true at all times in whatsoever thing they were entrusted. Yea, they were men of truth and soberness." And why? "They had been taught to keep the commandments of God and to walk uprightly before him" (53:17–21).

Truly, these young men are a bright spot in an otherwise grim and disheartening period for the Nephite faithful who are besieged on every side. Helaman reports in an epistle to the valiant, freedom-loving Captain Moroni that cities are being lost and that Nephite troops are "depressed in body as well as in spirit, for they had fought valiantly by day and toiled by night to maintain their cities," suffering "great afflictions of every kind" (Alma 56:16). They are lifted and reinvigorated by the arrival of "those sons of mine," Helaman says, finding in them "great hopes and much joy" (56:17). Furthermore, "the fathers of those my two thousand sons" brought "many provisions" for the Nephite forces (56:27).

Helaman continues to sing the praises of these extraordinary young men whom he repeatedly refers to as his sons, saying that "never had I seen so great courage, nay, not amongst all the Nephites" (56:45). Helaman reports that when he asked them if they were ready to go to battle, they responded in the affirmative, though they had never before borne arms: "Father [for so they called Helaman], behold our God is with us, and he will not suffer that we should fall" (56:46). As Helaman says,

> They did not fear death; and they did think more upon the liberty of their fathers than they did upon their lives; yea, they had been taught by their mothers, that if they did not doubt, God would deliver them.
>
> And they rehearsed unto me the words of their mothers, saying: We do not doubt our mothers knew it. (56:47–48)

That passage is especially dear to me, for obvious reasons.

Helaman emphasizes over and over again the power of the teachings these young sons received in their homes, and his affection for them is indeed that of a father. And all of them—not one slacker in the bunch—are "firm and undaunted." They "obey and observe to perform every word of command with exactness; yea, and even according to their faith it was done unto them" (Alma 57:20–21), for "not one soul of them . . . did perish" (57:25). Helaman himself "remember[s] the words which they said unto [him] that their mothers had taught them" (57:21). He attributes their amazing survival, despite many wounds, "to the miraculous power of God, because of their exceeding faith in that which they had been taught to believe" (57:26). His praise is nearly endless as he says again, "they are young, and their minds are firm, and they do put their trust in God continually" (57:27).

These "sons of the people of Ammon," Helaman repeats, "are strict to remember the Lord their God from day to day; yea, they do observe to keep his statutes, and his judgments, and his commandments continually; and their faith is strong in the prophecies concerning that which is to come" (Alma 58:39–40). The fact that Helaman speaks so often of these young men, and in such glowing terms, suggests just how extraordinary they were. After all, this letter is a military report of conditions, concerns, and needs on the battlefront from an officer to his commander.

Clearly, the steadfast faith of these youths is rooted in the unwavering faith of their parents. And the faith of their parents is rooted in their generation's repentance and conversion on being taught the gospel of Jesus Christ by Ammon and his fellow missionaries. The pure love of Christ began to blossom among the Nephites' former enemies when Lamoni and his father were touched first by Ammon's charity and faith and then by gospel truths. These powerful kings humbly opened their minds and hearts, and then their countries, to the word of God, and their people responded. Homes where faith and obedience were lovingly practiced and taught produced young men of great faith, courage, and loyalty.

Again, the example of charity, the word of truth, and the constancy of righteous living create a miracle. It is a constancy that the Nephites as a people might profitably have learned from their Lamanite brothers and sisters. I should make clear, however, that in spite of the vacillating that characterizes the Nephite people throughout much of the record, there is always a solid, if sometimes small, core of enduring Nephite faithful. They know themselves to be a covenant people, and they strive always to keep the Lord's commandments and keep the church functioning. Among them are those charged with responsibility for the records, and for teaching the gospel of Jesus Christ and prophesying of his birth and ministry. And after he comes, the faithful continue to teach and warn, right to the end.

A SIDE NOTE ON CHARITY—
HELAMAN, CAPTAIN MORONI, AND PAHORAN

In the same letter to Captain Moroni in which he sings the praises of the courageous young Ammonites, Helaman also describes the dire situation of Nephite troops in the field. They are not only short-handed, but they are also suffering from lack of food and other supplies. As a result of seeming neglect by the central government in Zarahemla, Nephite cities recently retaken have been lost again, and the future looks bleak for the weakened, starving army. Helaman closes his very long letter humbly, not wishing to make unfair assumptions about why support has not come. He does, however, raise the possibility that "some faction in the government" has chosen not to assist his men in their efforts to preserve the liberty of the Nephite people. Helaman is a soft-spoken man, slow to anger, not vengeful at all—apologetic, in fact, for further burdening Moroni. How many of us could say in such circumstances that, finally, "it mattereth not—we trust God will deliver us . . . out of the hands of our enemies" (58:37).

Moroni, having written once to Pahoran, the Nephite chief judge, and seemingly been ignored, writes again. Now he is boiling mad. Circumstances could hardly be worse. On the home front, Moroni is battling the Nephite "king-men" who wish to overthrow the democratic government and establish a monarchy, with themselves in power. And in the outer reaches of the country, Lamanites under the leadership of apostate Nephites are attacking Nephite cities. All it takes to send Moroni into a rage is the slightest suggestion that now Pahoran and his colleagues might have defected. Moroni, faithful and true, but scarcely full of charity at the moment, fires off a second letter to Pahoran, a scathing letter this time, demanding "to know the cause of this exceedingly great neglect" (Alma 60:6).

He quickly warms to his subject, boldly asking, "Can you think to sit upon your thrones in a state of thoughtless stupor, while your enemies are spreading the work of death around you?" (60:7). This is the governor of the land he is addressing, remember, but Moroni holds nothing back. And the more he writes, the angrier he gets, accusing Pahoran of deliberately withholding provisions and warning him that "the blood of thousands shall come upon your heads for vengeance" (60:10). The government, he contends, is not only slothful, but for all he knows, "ye yourselves are seeking authority," and may well be "traitors to your country" (60:14, 18). Moroni goes on in this manner for thirty-six verses, and as his temperature gauge rises, so does his rhetoric. Having pretty much convinced himself that Pahoran and his associates "love . . . glory and the vain things of the world," and "trample [the laws of God] under your feet" (60:32–33), Moroni threatens to march to Zarahemla "and smite [them] with the sword" (60:30). It will be "the sword of justice" which "shall fall upon [them] and visit [them] even to [their] utter destruction" (60:29).

Whew! Now, we admire Moroni, and we know him to be a noble and forthright man (if short-tempered at times) who loves his people and their liberty and his God more than life. Nevertheless, I have to ask myself how I would respond to such a letter, a very unfair letter as it turns out. A letter written in the heat of battle, without benefit of the facts. Pahoran, having finally received the second letter, writes to Moroni explaining that he has been forced to flee Zarahemla, which has been taken over by the king-men. Very likely, he narrowly escaped with his life. In the meantime he has been rallying what forces he can to assist in "the defence of their country and their freedom" (Alma 61:6).

But then, Pahoran responds to what became a very personal attack from his chief captain and one-time friend. Does he respond with like anger? Does he berate Moroni for his unfair, hasty, and even damning accusations and threats? No. Listen to his words and stand in awe at such magnanimity: "And now, in your epistle you have censured me, but it mattereth not; I am not angry, but do rejoice in the greatness of your heart" (61:9). Repeat those words aloud: "It mattereth not; I am not angry, but do rejoice in the greatness of your heart." He says further, "I do joy in receiving your epistle" (61:19), for it has given him a sense of how they should proceed. His closing words, "my beloved brother, Moroni" (61:21), say it all. This indeed is charity, the pure love of Christ, shown under great duress and wrong. This is a sterling example of the turning of the other cheek. This is the Savior's way.

And so, I include Pahoran's answer to Moroni's charges as one of those bright moments in the Book of Mormon. True, it is not a moment of conversion from disbelief to faith, but a sweet moment of utter forgiving, of refusing to take offense, of absorbing a wrong rather than striking back. We are told that Moroni's immediate response to Pahoran's letter was to "take courage," and rejoice in "the faithfulness of Pahoran" (Alma 62:1). Together they restore democracy in Zarahemla and peace in the land. I can only assume that Moroni rejoiced to learn that Pahoran was faithful to the trust placed in him and gratefully accepted his friend's forgiveness.

VIII

LAMANITE CONVERSIONS:
IN THE LANDS OF ZARAHEMLA AND NEPHI

We are told that the lengthy wars involving Moroni and Helaman hardened the hearts of many, yet softened the hearts of others who were humbled by their afflictions (see Alma 62:41). The church is re-established, and peace and prosperity return. But all too soon an "exceedingly great pride" enters the hearts of some as they acquire riches of the world (Helaman 3:33–34, 36). Predictably, dissensions arise in the church and contentions grow among the people. Sadly, this pride and dissent lead to war, great loss of life and lands, and the appearance of such ambitious scoundrels as Kishkumen and Gadianton. The record attributes the terrible decline in large part to the overt rejection of charity as the prideful rich oppress the poor, "withholding their food from the hungry, withholding their clothing from the naked, and smiting their humble brethren upon the cheek." These practices go hand in hand with mockery of sacred things and all manner of evildoing (Helaman 4:12).

With the passing generations, Helaman's son (Alma's grandson), also named Helaman, dies, and his son Nephi becomes chief judge. But as wickedness escalates, and the "stiffnecked people" Nephi is attempting to govern become the majority, he elects to yield the judgment seat and follow the path taken by his great-grandfather Alma. He vows "to preach the word of God all the remainder of his days, and his brother Lehi also" (Helaman 5:4). These two brothers, remembering the words of their father, go forth teaching in Nephite cities across the "land southward; and from thence into the land of Zarahemla, among the Lamanites" and the Nephite dissenters who had joined with the Lamanites (5:16–17). It is there, and in the land of Nephi, which has long remained the center of the Lamanite nation, that great miracles occur once again.

The record does not dwell at length on the conversions in and around Zarahemla but notes that the two brothers "had what they should speak given unto them." They teach "with such great power and authority" that they astonish the Lamanites and convince them of the truth of their message. Indeed, "there were eight thousand of the Lamanites . . . baptized unto repentance" in that area (5:18–19). We can only try to imagine the joy of those conversions, with inspired teachers bearing witness of Christ and his truths, and inspired listeners embracing those truths heart and soul.

Things look rather grim, however, when Nephi and Lehi enter the land of Nephi, once again home to their sworn Lamanite enemies. The brothers are cast into prison by a Lamanite army where they languish "many days without food." And then their captors appear at "the prison to take them that they might slay them" (5:22). At that point, heaven intervenes and the miracles begin. What do the astonished captors see but "Nephi and Lehi . . . encircled about as if by fire." The would-be executioners "durst not lay their hands upon them for fear lest they should be burned," and yet "Nephi and Lehi were not burned." The record repeats the incredible truth that "they were as standing in the midst of fire and were not burned." Aware of what is happening, "that they were encircled about with a pillar of fire, and that it burned them not, their hearts did take courage" (5:23–24). The Lamanites, in turn, are "struck dumb with amazement" (5:25). And this is only the beginning of miraculous events that nearly defy description.

Nephi and Lehi "stand forth and [begin] to speak," assuring those present that "it is God that has shown unto you this marvelous thing," and that they will not be allowed to harm the prisoners (5:26). As they speak, the earth shakes "exceedingly," causing the prison walls to wobble. The murderous Lamanites and Nephite dissenters are "overshadowed with a cloud of darkness, and an awful solemn fear came upon them" (5:28). A voice speaks from above, the Lord's voice, commanding them to repent and forbidding them to harm his servants whom he has sent to deliver his word. "It was not a voice of thunder," nor "of a great tumultuous noise," but rather "a still voice of perfect mildness, as if it had been a whisper, and it did pierce even to the very soul" (5:29–30). Then the earth shakes wildly again, and the prison walls seem "about to tumble to the earth" (5:31). Once more the Lord's voice demands repentance and warns against harm to his servants, and once more the earth and the prison walls shake (5:32).

This is the sort of thing that makes an impression, especially when it occurs in the midst of thick darkness. And now, try to envision the scene when the Lord's voice comes yet again, only this time speaking "marvelous words which cannot be uttered by man." The walls and the earth tremble and shake in response, and the warriors, still enveloped in the dark cloud, are frozen with terror (5:33–34). The Lord has their undivided attention. It so happens that a "Nephite by birth" is among them, a man named Aminidab who "had once belonged to the church of God." He is given the power to discern "through the cloud of darkness the faces of Nephi and Lehi." He perceives that "they did shine exceedingly, even as the faces of angels." Moreover, he sees "that they did lift their eyes to heaven," as though they were "talking or lifting their voices to some being whom they beheld" (5:35–37).

Aminidab turns to the "multitude" at the prison, crying to them to "look." They, too, receive power to see and they "behold the faces of Nephi and Lehi" (5:37). The miracle doubles and redoubles as those present ask Aminidab whom the brothers are addressing. He answers, "They do converse with the angels of God" (5:39). Sufficiently humbled, the people are eager to listen, and they ask what they can do to be rescued from the dark cloud. Aminidab well knows what it will take and he reminds them of the teachings of Alma and Amulek and Zeezrom— all three, we remember, having been changed in their hearts. (Apparently these people had the Nephite records among them.) "You must repent," Aminidab says, "and cry unto the voice, even until ye shall have faith in Christ" (5:40–41). They do so, crying out until the cloud disperses.

Then they, and we, witness a glorious moment. As the cloud disappears, these repentant cutthroats see themselves "encircled about, yea every soul, by a pillar of fire" (5:43). I simply must quote these next verses, they are so filled with light and wonder. Take yourself to that prison and experience the incomparable blessing bestowed from heaven on these amazed, changed people:

> And Nephi and Lehi were in the midst of them; yea, they were

encircled about; yea, they were as if in the midst of a flaming fire, yet it did harm them not, . . . and they were filled with that joy which is unspeakable and full of glory.

And behold, the Holy Spirit of God did come down from heaven and did enter into their hearts, and they were filled as if with fire, and they could speak forth marvelous words.

And . . . there came a voice unto them, yea, a pleasant voice, as if it were a whisper, saying:

Peace, peace be unto you because of your faith in my Well Beloved, who was from the foundation of the world. (5:44–47)

Read the passage again, aloud, and recreate the scene in your mind. Hear the voice of the Father, speaking of his divine Son, addressing this group of "about three hundred souls," who are then blessed to see "the heavens open; and angels came down out of heaven and ministered unto them" (5:48–49). I remember the concern of a later Moroni, the last surviving Nephite, that latter-day readers would mock at the record because the keepers of that record lacked polish in their writing. As I read passages like the one above, passages that literally take my breath away, I wish I could tell this dear Moroni how they touch me and enliven my faith. The Lord knows that the words will reach some of us with a power Moroni could not anticipate in his time of agony and grief. A loving Lord gently assures his faithful servant that only "fools mock" at such things, and any who do "shall mourn" one day (Ether 12:26).

The awestruck witnesses to these wondrous happenings then "go forth" ministering and "declaring throughout all the regions round about all the things which they had heard and seen," convincing "the more part of the Lamanites" of their truth (Helaman 5:50). But the miracles do not cease. First, the converted warriors and their country-men "lay down their weapons of war"; second, they lay down "their hatred"; and third, they lay down "the traditions of their fathers" (5:51). Think of the magnitude of these willing sacrifices. Giving up weaponry is something indeed, but perhaps nothing compared with giving up cherished hatred and even more cherished traditions. As if such sac-rifices were not enough, these transformed people also "yield up unto the Nephites the lands of their possessions" (5:52). Simply incredible. And so again we see the fruits of the great change that is wrought when hearts are touched and moved upon by the Spirit. This is the pure love of Christ in action.

As with the much earlier conversions of Lamoni and his father and their people, this generation of Lamanites also remains constant and true. Moreover, the record tells us that the righteousness of these people "did exceed that of the Nephites, because of their firmness and their steadiness in the faith" (Helaman 6:1). In contrast, "many" of their Nephite contemporaries "had become hardened and impenitent and grossly wicked," rejecting "the word of God and all the preaching and prophesying which did come among them" (6:2). There is much rejoicing among the church faithful at these conversions and much fellowshipping. The Lamanites even begin teaching the Nephites in the land of Zarahemla and elsewhere.

Thus, peace reigns for a time, a very short time. But then—crash. Cezoram, the Nephite chief judge is murdered, as is his son who succeeds him. In the span of two years, from "great joy and peace" (6:14), the Nephite people start tumbling into wickedness. No longer occupied by war and bloodshed, they begin "to set their hearts upon their riches," to "seek to get gain." And why? "That they might be lifted up one above another" (6:17). I find it very significant that these Nephites "turn unto their own ways" and become so self-engrossed that they "build up unto themselves idols of their gold and their silver" (6:31). (Does any of this sound familiar in our own era?) There it is again, that old nemesis—pride and status-seeking, the rejection of charity.

This, unfortunately, opens the door to the opportunistic Gadiantons who appear right on schedule, and "the more part of the Nephites . . . unite with those bands of robbers" (6:21). They "build them up and support them, . . . and partake of their spoils" (6:38). The converted Lamanites, however, unlike their capricious brothers, "use every means in their power to destroy [the Gadiantons] off the face of the earth" (6:20). Why, why, are so many of the Nephites so inconstant? How is it that the Lamanites, when once brought to faith, rarely falter? It is certainly telling that even as the Nephites "grow in wickedness and abominations, . . . the Lamanites . . . grow exceedingly in the knowledge of their God." They "keep his statutes and commandments," and they "walk in truth and uprightness before him" (6:34). Consequently, "the Spirit of the Lord began to withdraw from the Nephites," and "the Lord began to pour out his Spirit upon the Lamanites" (6:35–36).

When Nephi returns to Zarahemla, he finds "Gadianton robbers filling the judgment-seats" and doing whatever they please (Helaman 7:4–5). Speaking from a tower in his garden to puzzled listeners who have gathered, he calls on them to repent. He specifically alludes to their thirst for "gain" and their desire "to be praised of men" (7:21). Their hearts, he says, are "hardened" and set "upon the riches and the vain things of this world." For such they stop at nothing, whether it be murder, plunder, or anything else (7:18, 21). They have allowed "pride . . . to enter [their] hearts," which pride has "lifted" them "beyond" the good because of their "exceedingly great riches" (7:26). Nephi holds up to them the example of the Lamanites who have embraced the truth, who "are more righteous" than the Nephites who received "that great knowledge" and "sinned against" it. "Therefore," he says, "the Lord will be merciful unto them," and "will lengthen out their days and increase their seed," even if the Nephites should fail to repent and "be utterly destroyed" (7:24).

This Nephi is such a righteous man that the Lord has given him extraordinary power. Whatever he asks will be granted, whether it be to "smite the earth with famine, and with pestilence, and destruction," or to "rent" the temple "in twain," or to make a mountain "become smooth" (Helaman 10:6, 8–9). Unfortunately, the "great miracle which Nephi had done in telling them concerning the death of the chief judge" (10:13) makes no lasting impression. The Nephites close their ears, "harden their hearts" (10:13, 15), and return to their old ways.

But another miracle is granted to this splendid man. When the people "revile against him" and try to take him and "cast him into prison," he is miraculously "conveyed away out of the midst of them," through "the Spirit" and by "the power of God" (10:15–16). The frustrated sinners are unable to touch him as he goes "forth in the Spirit, from multitude to multitude, declaring the word of God" to "all the people" (10:17). They refuse to listen—no surprise there—and so he asks the Lord to send a famine to divert their attention from killing each other. Starvation and the deaths of "thousands" bring them around (Helaman 11:6–7), and Nephi asks the Lord to end the famine. He does, and for a time, the church thrives and the people rejoice in peace and prosperity. In that small window of peace, "the more part of the people, both the Nephites and the Lamanites, did belong to the church," with Nephi, Lehi, and other faithful men "having many revelations daily" (11:21, 23).

The peace doesn't last. All too soon humility reverts to pride once more among the Nephites. Another round of dissent and powerful Gadianton uprisings ensues, followed by remembrance and then again forgetfulness, and a people who "wax stronger and stronger in their pride" (11:37). It is a dizzying roller coaster ride that leaves my head spinning. I am continually amazed at how many times the Lord is willing to forgive and bless his people, no matter what they have done, if they humbly repent and come to him. Anyone who sees him as a harsh, unforgiving God has not read the Book of Mormon with any real understanding. How he must ache at the short memories of mortals who use his outpouring of blessings to feed pride, ambition, and hate.

I can't help noting yet another difference between the lasting faith of the Lamanite people, once they accept Christ as their Lord, and the slip-sliding faith of the Nephite people generally. The Lamanites are often brought to repentance and enduring faith simply by hearing the words of truth taught to them. That is true today also, in the lands of Polynesia and Latin America. Sometimes a heavenly manifestation launches the teaching in Book of Mormon times, but not always. Even so, thousands are ready to repent and believe the words of the testifiers of such events. And the faith of Lamoni and his father, we remember, preceded the miracles they experienced. All too typically, however, the prideful, hard-hearted Nephites don't repent until they are forced to their knees—by war, by suffering, by famine, by pestilence, and by colossal earth-shattering events.

In the whole of Helaman 12, which appears to be inserted commentary, Mormon draws lessons from the events he has just summarized from the record. He is speaking directly to us. I can feel his great earnestness, the pleading in his voice—and I note that, as in other places, he uses the first person "I" near the end of this discourse (Helaman 12:25). Chapter 12 becomes both a sermon and a prayer, which he closes with a decisive "amen" (12:26).

Discouragement is evident in Mormon's voice as he reminds us of the "great nothingness of the children of men" who are, in fact, "less than the dust of the earth" (12:7). The earth, after all, responds to the voice and will of God while these prideful Nephites do not (see 12:8). A sorrowing Mormon has seen the pattern over and over again, and he will yet see it completely destroy his people. "How quick to be lifted up in pride," he says, and "how quick to boast" are these forgetful Nephites.

So caught up in their own self-importance are they that "they do not desire that the Lord their God, who hath created them, should rule and reign over them." They "set at naught his counsels, and they will not that he should be their guide" (12:5–6). There is no love in them, neither for God nor for their fellow mortals. No wonder Mormon would speak so earnestly about charity in a sermon to his own people (see earlier discussion of Moroni 7).

Into this setting of lapsed Nephite believers comes Samuel, the Lamanite prophet. He is a powerful example of the staying power of Lamanite faith. We saw the courage of Ammon, his brothers, and others who went alone into hostile territories and wrought marvelous conversions among earlier generations of Lamanite people. We have seen it more recently when the valiant brothers, Nephi and Lehi, took the gospel to multitudes of their Lamanite brethren. Samuel is a product of this last Lamanite conversion. It is now approximately twenty-four years since that great event and just six years before Jesus Christ will be born into mortality. While the Nephites have cycled in and out of faith during this period, the Lamanites have held firm.

Samuel arrives in Zarahemla where, unlike Samuel's people who "observe strictly to keep the commandments of God," the Nephites "remain . . . in great wickedness" (Helaman 13:1). Samuel's mission from the Lord is to bring these people to repentance, and he speaks boldly. The Lord is willing to give them yet another chance. Standing atop the wall around the city, Samuel repeatedly condemns the Nephites for their hard hearts and their pride, and he prophesies impending destruction and a curse on the land if they continue in this path. As Samuel describes them, they are the very antithesis of charity. It is their riches they remember rather than their God, and they "swell with great pride, unto boasting, and unto great swelling, envyings, strifes, malice, persecutions, and murders" (13:22). The pure love of Christ is nowhere to be found, for they have "cast out the prophets," "mock[ed] them, and cast stones at them," and slain them (13:24).

The whole of chapter 13 (thirty-nine verses!) is given to the warning words of Samuel, this inspired Lamanite who risks his life in an effort to save the souls of those who don't wish to be reminded of their iniquities and danger. But then, he turns to prophecy of another kind, wondrous prophecy of the miraculous signs in the heavens that will precede and herald the birth of Christ the Lord, and also the frightening cosmic and earthly signs of his death. Samuel earnestly pleads with these Nephites to "remember, remember" that they are free to "choose life or death" (Helaman 14:30–31). And he begs them, calling them his "beloved brethren" (Helaman 15:1), to repent. He reminds them that his people, the Lamanites, were once hated of the Lord because of their iniquities, but "the more part of them are in the path of their duty, and they do walk circumspectly before God, and they do observe to keep his commandments and his statutes and his judgments" (15:5).

Samuel speaks of the "faith and repentance" that have led to "a change of heart" (15:7) in his people, whom the Lord will greatly bless for "their steadfastness" when they come to believe, and for "their firmness when they are once enlightened" (15:10). I'm sure Samuel's listeners are not exactly pleased to hear him sing the praises of their righteous erstwhile enemies. In the true spirit of current Nephite brotherhood, many not only refuse to believe Samuel's words, but they also begin casting stones and shooting arrows at him. The Spirit protects him, however, and he escapes. Some of the Nephites come around, if only for a time, but most do not. Even the glorious manifestations that multiply as the Savior's birth draws near do not have a lasting effect. Listen to the wonders that all but a few of these people turn their backs on:

> There were great signs given unto the people, and wonders; and the words of the prophets began to be fulfilled.
>
> And angels did appear unto men, wise men, and did declare unto them glad tidings of great joy; thus in this year the scriptures began to be fulfilled. (Helaman 16:13–14)

These hard-hearted, self-centered folks prefer to rely on "their own strength and . . . their own wisdom" (16:15), arguing "that it is not reasonable that such a being as Christ shall come." And anyway, why wouldn't he "show himself" in this land as well as in the land of Jerusalem? they ask (16:18–19). The doubters have become subject to Satan's influence, "imagin[ing] up in their hearts" things "which were foolish and vain; . . . notwithstanding the signs and wonders . . . and the many miracles" they had witnessed (16:22–23). Minds are closed, and hearts are harder than ever. This is a self-indulgent, prideful crowd. They will learn the hard way.

PART THREE

Climactic EVENTS

I

3 NEPHI: SIGNS, WONDERS, AND APOSTASY

The Nephi we came to know in the book of Helaman, as a dedicated missionary and then as prophet and keeper of the record, disappears, "and whither he went, no man knoweth" (3 Nephi 1:3). This great-grandson of the younger Alma departs in the same manner as had his noble progenitor generations earlier, leaving no trace. But we remember him as the prophet who was so righteous that the Lord granted him unlimited power, knowing full well that this Nephite leader would never ask for anything that would be contrary to divine will. An inserted heading titled "The Prophecy of Nephi, the Son of Helaman" tells us that chapters 7 through 16 of the book of Helaman were abridged from the record kept by this remarkable man.

In many ways, the book of 3 Nephi is the climactic book of the entire Book of Mormon. If the abridger of the record in our hands felt compelled to move rather swiftly through the portion named after Helaman (grandson of Alma), perhaps it was because he had in his hands the record kept by Helaman's grandson, named Nephi after his father. With the departure of the elder Nephi, the younger Nephi bears the responsibility for recording the New World events and cosmic signs that precede and accompany the Savior's birth and death in the Old World.

More than that, he is appointed to document the marvelous arrival and the stirring ministry of the resurrected Lord in the New World. This man takes part in these events, the chosen disciple and recorder of the words and actions of the risen Christ, a huge responsibility. There is an immediacy about his account, perhaps even more so than in many

New Testament accounts, because he was present as a living witness. How blessed we are to have a record, abridged though it be, of these things. We are especially blessed because the New Testament, focusing as it wonderfully does on the mortal ministry of Jesus, contains precious few details of the Savior's appearances in the Holy Land after his Resurrection.

The first chapter of 3 Nephi introduces us briefly to the man who was destined to be called, not only to keep the record, but to head the church which Christ himself would establish personally. Surely, he was appointed for this time and this calling. As the year approaches when Jesus will be born of Mary, "the prophecies of the prophets began to be fulfilled more fully; for there began to be greater signs and greater miracles wrought among the people" (3 Nephi 1:4). While the faithful watch and pray and hope, the faithless "make a great uproar throughout the land" (1:7). The unbelievers are gratified as the days and years pass with no final indication of the Savior's birth. In fact, they set a deadline, of all things—a day by which the sign of his birth must be given or "all those who believed in those traditions should be put to death" (1:9). Imagine the utter gall of these uncharitable egotists who count themselves wiser than God! What kind of people would take it upon themselves to kill others if a prophecy is not fulfilled by a date they themselves set?

It is a distraught Nephi who bows to the earth, crying "mightily to his God in behalf of his people . . . who were about to be destroyed because of their faith" (1:11). He prays all day long, and then the Lord speaks to him, consoling him with these welcome words:

> Lift up your head and be of good cheer; for behold, the time is at hand, and on this night shall the sign be given, and on the morrow come I into the world, to show unto the world that I will fulfil all that which I have caused to be spoken by the mouth of my holy prophets. (1:13)

The Lord says it again: "And behold, the time is at hand, and this night shall the sign be given" (1:14). And indeed it is. The faithful are spared in this undeniable manifestation of divine grace. "At the going down of the sun there was no darkness" (1:15). Night arrives and it is light still. This gets the attention of many unbelievers, and they fall to earth, gripped with fear because they know the prophecies and have denied them. Indeed, "the sign which had been given was already at hand" (1:18).

What a gratifying moment this is for the humble who have kept the faith through the taunting and threats of their prideful countrymen. The language of the record is buoyant as it reports "that there was no darkness in all that night, but it was as light as though it was mid-day." And when the sun comes up "in the morning again, according to its proper order," witnesses to these events know that this is "the day that the Lord should be born" (1:19). Interestingly enough, the sun is not stopped in its normal course but sets and rises as always. The miracle of undimmed light throughout the night has nothing to do with the sun. The light comes from God himself, whose power is matchless. The record reminds us that these things were prophesied:

> And it had come to pass, yea, all things, every whit, according to the words of the prophets.
> And it came to pass also that a new star did appear, according to the word. (1:20–21)

And so, with these miraculous events, people are again repentant and are baptized. Peace follows, but it doesn't last. In just three short years, the Gadiantons, who infest the mountains and other secret places, become uncontrollable. They take to their murderous ways, and "many dissenters of the Nephites . . . flee unto them" (1:28). Even the Lamanites fall prey to the disease of dissent. As the Lamanite children grow to adulthood, the record says they "became for themselves" (1:29), an intriguing expression. I take it to mean that, unlike the devout young Lamanite sons who decades earlier went to battle to maintain their country's liberty, this prideful group of second-generation Lamanites are rather full of themselves. Rejecting the faith of their parents, they are "led away" by the "lyings" and "flattering words" of the apostate Zoramites (1:29).

Wars ensue, and the stalwart among the Nephites, led by commanders and a chief judge who have "the spirit of revelation and also prophecy" (3 Nephi 3:19), prevail because they refuse to mount an offense. Rather, after the preferred pattern of Captain Moroni, they fortify themselves in one place; then, through faith and prayer and defense alone, they defeat their Gadianton enemies. Having won the peace, they know boundless happiness, and they "break forth, all as one, in singing, and praising their God for the great thing which he had done for them, in preserving them" (3 Nephi 4:31). Hear their elation as they cry, "Hosanna to the Most High God. . . . Blessed be the name of the Lord God Almighty, the Most High God" (4:32). The record goes on to describe their thankful bliss:

> And their hearts were swollen with joy, unto the gushing out of many tears, because of the great goodness of God in delivering them out of the hands of their enemies; and they knew it was because of their repentance and their humility that they had been delivered from an everlasting destruction. (4:33)

What an experience, and what a lesson it holds for us about the joy and safety that come with humility and repentance. In chapter 5 Mormon inserts his own commentary, describing this lovely oasis of peace and harmony. Here again, the formula for peace is believing the words of Christ, as spoken by prophets; forsaking sin; serving God faithfully; and rejecting Gadiantonism and its creed forged in murder, lies, lust for power, and greed. Indeed, Gadiantonism is always the very opposite of faith in Christ, the opposite of charity, of pure love.

I find it noteworthy, too, that these spared and repentant people are willing to exercise the pure love of Christ toward any of their prisoners who "would repent of their sins and enter into a covenant that they would murder no more." These recent enemies are readily "set at liberty" (3 Nephi 5:4). We have noted that anciently such covenants were binding, but I still find this and previous such acts of charity quite amazing. Any prisoners who refuse to enter such a covenant are "punished according to the law" (5:5). If past experience is any indicator, I suspect that it is the Lamanite captives, rather than the Nephite apostates, who are most likely to have repented and sworn a covenant of peace. This idea is at least suggested in 3 Nephi 6 where, in a discussion of the return of Nephites to their lands, we read this:

> And they granted unto those robbers who had entered into a covenant to keep the peace of the land, *who were desirous to remain Lamanites*, lands, according to their numbers, that they might have, with their labors, wherewith to subsist upon; and thus they did establish peace in all the land. (3 Nephi 6:3, emphasis added)

And so, once again, the Nephites—when they are living righteously—extend a generous hand of love to their Lamanite brethren who have humbled themselves.

Prosperity returns with the return of peace. Cities are built and rebuilt, along with highways and roads. But guess what? Scarcely three years later, disputations disturb the peace as some of the moneyed folk are "lifted up unto pride and boastings," and "unto great persecutions." Charity is cast aside as "the people began to be distinguished by ranks, according to their riches and their chances for learning." The separation into classes is apparent, and some are left "ignorant because of their poverty," while others "receive great learning because of their riches" (6:10, 12). Succeeding verses speak repeatedly of pride, that great destroyer of equality, peace, and love. In stark contrast to the arrogant who persecute and rail against their humbler brethren are the meek and penitent, the persecuted and reviled. Truly charitable, they express the pure love of Christ by their actions as they turn the other cheek, refusing to revile their tormentors.

"And thus," the record says, "there became a great inequality in all the land." And what is the result of this "great inequality"? The record makes it quite clear. The church begins to crumble. Within a year, "the church was broken up in all the land." But there is an exception, as there seems always to be among these people. And that exception is, as we have come to expect, "a few of the Lamanites who were converted unto the true faith; and they would not depart from it, for they were firm, and steadfast, and immovable, willing with all diligence to keep the commandments of the Lord" (6:14). The more I ponder these things, the more I understand the Lord's great love for the Lamanite people, and the more I understand why they were promised that they would not be completely destroyed.

The speed with which things fall apart in the Nephite nation is breathtaking. Satan comes to power, and what are his weapons? "Pride," "iniquity," the temptation "to seek for power, and authority, and riches, and the vain things of the world" (6:15). It hardly seems possible that within three or four years of righteousness and peace, these people could have descended into "a state of awful wickedness" (6:17), but they have. Even so, the Lord is willing, still, to rescue the prideful sinners. "Men inspired from heaven" go forth "preaching and testifying boldly of the sins and iniquities of the people," and also of "the redemption which the Lord would make for his people, . . . the resurrection of Christ," and "his death and sufferings" (6:20).

The corrupt judges and lawyers are angered by the brave men who testify of Christ, potentially undermining the power of these evil officials. They conspire in arranging the secret deaths of the bold spokesmen for Christ, covenanting to protect each other as they "combine against all righteousness," and "against the people of the Lord." In the process, they "set at defiance the law and rights of their country." Always, secret combinations shut down any charitable impulses in those who embrace them. Scorning the humble and their faith, the conspirators' goal is "to destroy the governor, and to establish a king over the land," thereby shattering liberty (6:28–30). As it turns out, a king is not set on a throne, though a man named Jacob becomes a "king" of sorts over a band of rebels. But in under six years, most of the people have spurned righteousness, organized into tribes, stoned the prophets, and cast them out (see 3 Nephi 7:1–14).

The second half of 3 Nephi 7 paints a mixed picture. We have Nephi boldly teaching and ministering "with power and with great authority" (7:17) among those who have made a "quick return from righteousness unto their wickedness and abominations" (7:15). All too many of the people, driven by the "hardness of their hearts and the blindness of their minds" (7:16), hate him "because of his power" (7:20). What they can't abide is the fact that "he had greater power than they, for it were not possible that they could disbelieve his words" (7:18). So they know Nephi speaks truth, and they recognize his stalwart faith, but their envy fuels an immense pride and an unreasonable anger. These foolish people, so lately basking in love and peace, and even extending charity toward their former enemies, now turn again to the senseless behavior that will destroy them. The last thing they want to hear is a man of faith testifying of Christ, and the last thing they want to see is a man of faith performing miracles in the name of Christ.

Although circumstances prohibited Mormon from recording more of this great prophet's words, if we read carefully the chapters in 3 Nephi that make specific reference to him—notably 7, 11, and 23—we can more fully realize the magnitude of his mission and calling. He is also among the disciples whom Jesus addresses in other chapters, such as 15, 19, 27, and 28. And remember, it is this Nephi's record that Mormon is abridging here. As Mormon says, "all of" the marvelous things Nephi said and did "cannot be written, and a part of them would not suffice, therefore they are not written in this book" (7:17). Pause on that tantalizing phrase, "part of them would not suffice." Nephi's writings must have been splendid. What we have of the record leaves no doubt that the grace of heaven was with him, for he was "visited by angels and also the voice of the Lord" (7:15) long before Christ appears in person.[1]

Mormon says again that Nephi had such great "faith on the Lord Jesus Christ that angels did minister unto him daily" (7:18). Imagine—*daily* visits by angels! Not only that, but "even his brother did he raise from the dead, after he had been stoned and suffered death by the people" (7:19). This tiny reference, to a man's being stoned to death for his faith, speaks volumes about the moral state of these people. Nephi also performs "many more miracles, in the sight of the people, in the name of Jesus" (7:20). He casts out devils and heals the afflicted "of their sicknesses and their infirmities" (7:22). We are told that notwithstanding these miracles, "but few" are converted; still, those few are "visited by the power and Spirit of God" (7:21). The ones who are healed "show forth signs" and perform miracles also (7:22). Furthermore, as the time draws near when the mortal Jesus will die and the immortal Christ will arrive in the land of Nephites and Lamanites, men are ordained to the ministry, and "many" people are "baptized unto repentance" (7:25–26).

Truly, too often we forget this Nephi. I cling to the hope that one day I will read his words. He certainly merits a place in our minds and hearts alongside the other Nephis who preceded him, and the other great Book of Mormon prophets. Mormon adds his tribute to Nephi, calling him "a just man" and noting that "he truly did many miracles in the name of Jesus" (3 Nephi 8:1).

---

1. I find it interesting that in teaching these people about scattered Israel and about their own place in the prophecies, Jesus specifically says that "the Gentiles should not at any time hear my voice," that his only manifestation to them would be "by the Holy Ghost." But you, he says to his people in the New World, "have both heard my voice, and seen me; and ye are my sheep, and ye are numbered among those whom the Father hath given me" (3 Nephi 15:23-24). In light of this, it should not surprise us to read his words spoken out of the heavens, and in person, among Nephite and Lamanite peoples.

II

3 Nephi: The Great Cataclysm and the Interim

Soon enough, at the crucifixion of Jesus in the Old World, cataclysmic destruction is visited on the peoples of the New World. The wicked are wiped out by thunderous events that sink entire cities in the sea, burn or bury others, and topple still others. The earth splits apart, and blinding darkness covers the whole land for three days. But the more righteous are spared to witness the most glorious of events ever experienced by ordinary mortals in the New World or anywhere else. The resurrected Lord comes to bless and teach these stricken people.

Let's consider for a moment the meaning and significance of the terrifying destruction in Book of Mormon lands that marks the crucifixion of Jesus Christ in Biblical lands. It is almost beyond comprehension to many of us. Some in our world, however, have been given a real taste of what these ancient peoples experienced. In recent years gigantic tsunamis, earthquakes, hurricanes, floods, volcanic eruptions, tornados, and the like have visited immense destruction and death on various peoples of the earth. Add to those things the wars, disease, and starvation that have brought whole nations to their knees, and we know that the human family is no stranger to suffering.

Nevertheless, I wonder if today's tragedies compare with the wholesale destruction and terrifying darkness witnessed "in the thirty and fourth year, in the first month, on the fourth day of the month" (3 Nephi 8:5) among Book of Mormon peoples. I wonder what it might take to wrench us, at least those of us still untouched by major disaster, from our individual and collective complacency, pride, and selfishness? What cataclysmic events might be required to impel us to wholehearted, complete repentance? More particularly, what might it take to bring us to embrace our fellow mortals—all of them, including those whose world views (and politics) are different from ours—in the pure love of Christ?

The physical devastation and loss of life accompanying the three hours of earth-splitting events were certainly frightening enough, but perhaps no worse than the three days of rumblings and vaporous blackness that followed, a thick darkness pierced only by the wailing and mourning of survivors. Repeatedly the record states that there was no light at all—nothing. No fire, no candles, no lights visible in the heavens. I'll not detail the destruction. You can read of it and weep as I have.

And yet, terrifying as these events are, I can see a purpose in them. I see a miracle and even a blessing. Here we have a great cleansing, a necessary cleansing, a purifying of both the land and its people, in preparation for the coming of the Great Redeemer, the resurrected Son of God, to the western hemisphere. Cleansing must precede the blessings and teachings that will come at his hand, in order that his church be established and the new covenant implemented. We should not forget that it is the more righteous of his people who are spared to receive his very person, his blessings and teachings. The survivors, and the land itself, are blessed with a fresh start. For these people, it is new life, new opportunity, and a personal experience with the Creator of the world on which they stand. It is a lesson for us, too, assuring us that nothing divinely ordained is done without purpose or love.

As we contemplate the purpose of the great cataclysm in Lehite lands, we might consider the possibility that something similar awaits us. Events described in 3 Nephi 8 might help prepare us for, or even give us a preview of, what lies ahead. As we well know, another cleansing has been prophesied, one of frightening magnitude. And like the cleansing experienced by Book of Mormon peoples, the next one will also prepare the earth to receive the risen Lord. Only this time, the whole earth will know of it—the magnificent Second Coming.

The ministry of Christ that followed the cleansing in Nephite lands brought two centuries of peace among the survivors and their posterity—peace such as had never been seen on earth for any significant length of time. We are promised that the cleansing yet to come will initiate a millennium of peace beyond human imagining. We should not forget, either, that even in the midst of rubble and death, these early peoples began very soon to know a joy they would not trade for anything. I suspect not even in exchange for lost cities.

Take yourself there; experience what it would be like to hear his voice, speaking out of the darkness, pleading with you to "return unto me, and repent of your sins, and be converted, that I may heal you." Hear him promise that "if ye will come unto me ye shall have eternal life," that "mine arm of mercy is extended towards you, and whosoever will come, him will I receive; and blessed are those who come unto me" (3 Nephi 9:13–14).

Having spoken these sweet words of invitation, the Savior then tells his stricken people, in powerful language, who he is, what his mission is, and what is required of them if he is to receive them. He speaks with authority, with meaning no one could misunderstand. Read these passages aloud slowly, absorbing them into your mind and soul. First, his identity and his mission:

> Behold, I am Jesus Christ the Son of God. I created the heavens and the earth, and all things that in them are. I was with the Father from the beginning. I am in the Father, and the Father in me; and in me hath the Father glorified his name.
>
> I came unto my own, and my own received me not. And the scriptures concerning my coming are fulfilled.
>
> And as many as have received me, to them have I given to become the sons of God; . . . by me redemption cometh, and in me is the law of Moses fulfilled.
>
> I am the light and life of the world. I am Alpha and Omega, the beginning and the end. (9:15–18)

And then he tells what he requires of these people, because blood sacrifices and burnt offerings are no longer acceptable. This is what he requires of us, too:

> And ye shall offer for a sacrifice unto me a broken heart and a contrite spirit. And whoso cometh unto me with a broken heart and a contrite spirit, him will I baptize with fire and with the Holy Ghost, even as the Lamanites, because of their faith in me at the time of their conversion, were baptized with fire and with the Holy

Ghost, and they knew it not. (9:20)[1]

Pause with me here. The Lord is holding up the Lamanites as the example to follow, the example of pure faith. In the days of Ammon, these humbled people came to their Savior repenting, with hearts changed and a lasting desire to live in peace and love according to his will. All rancor and selfishness had vanished, and the Holy Ghost descended upon them, even though at the time they didn't fully understand the experience.

And now the Lord restates his mission and his promise, to the survivors he is addressing and to us:

> Behold, I have come unto the world to bring redemption unto the world, to save the world from sin.
>
> Therefore, whoso repenteth and cometh unto me as a little child, him will I receive, for of such is the kingdom of God. Behold, for such have I laid down my life, and have taken it up again; therefore repent, and come unto me ye ends of the earth, and be saved. (9:21–22)

We might learn several things from these passages. Here, as elsewhere, the Lord assures his listeners that a sophisticated understanding of gospel mysteries is not required for redemption. What is required, first and foremost, is sincere repentance, humility, and an earnest desire to know him. The Lord makes it clear that he will "receive" only those who become like the repentant Lamanites and guileless children. I note that it is "of such" that he says "the kingdom of God" is comprised. And it is "for such" that he has "laid down" his life. These, we must remember, are *his* words, spoken by him for his immediate audience and recorded for us. We can't escape the fact that the Lord pointedly addresses not only the Nephites and Lamanites engulfed in frightening darkness, but "ye ends of the earth." That last phrase seems to include every mortal of every place and time, be the dark vapors surrounding them actual or figurative.

When the voice from heaven ceases, the people respond in stunned silence to what they have heard. After several hours the Lord speaks

---

1. Does this passage suggest that in taking the Sacrament we renew not only our "baptism by water" covenants, but also our "baptism by fire" covenants—specifically the offering of "a broken heart and a contrite spirit"?

again, reminding them that his desire has always been to gather Israel to him. These stricken people mourn in darkness three long days, for their lost loved ones and their lost cities. But with the dispersing of darkness and the quieting of the earth, "their mourning was turned into joy, and their lamentations into the praise and thanksgiving unto the Lord Jesus Christ, their Redeemer" (3 Nephi 10:10). Having been fully chastened—and remember, only the more righteous were spared—they are ready to take up a life of faith and hope. A very sober Mormon now speaks directly to us: "whoso readeth, let him understand; he that hath the scriptures, let him search them" (10:14). He deliberately reminds us of prophecies now fulfilled, and he prepares us for the account of the arrival and ministry of Jesus Christ among "the people of Nephi" and "those who had been called Lamanites" (10:18–19). Note the phrase "had been called"; it refers to the past, not the present. "The people of Nephi" plainly refers to persons of the covenant and not to ancestry—and all these people qualify. The Savior will now tolerate no semantic separation into Nephites and Lamanites.

III

3 Nephi: The Risen Lord Comes

The arrival of the resurrected Christ among his people in the New World inaugurates the most glorious period in all of Nephite history. It is a period of miracles, of learning, of joy, of spiritual growth, of peace, and of pure love that has probably never been matched before or since. I truly believe that this time of divine instruction and bliss could not have occurred if a great cleansing had not worked its transforming power among the people who were there to receive the Lord into their hearts and lives. Picture a good number of the faithful gathering about the temple in Bountiful now, "marveling and wondering one with another," and "conversing about this Jesus Christ, of whom the sign had been given concerning his death" (3 Nephi 11:1–2). As they talk, they again hear a voice from heaven, a different voice, soft and piercing to the very soul. A voice that "cause[s] their hearts to burn" (11:3).

Twice the voice speaks and they fail to understand. But the third time, they open their spiritual ears, and then they understand the words, if not the full meaning of those words. It is the voice of the Father, introducing the Son. Even so, when a Man clothed in white descends, they assume he is an angel. They are wrong, of course, and immediately the Savior announces who he is. I have noticed that in speaking to mortals, the true God always identifies himself, while the imposter, Satan, never does. The deceiver always tries to fool us; the true God never deceives. Reaching out his hand, the Savior says,

> Behold, I am Jesus Christ, whom the prophets testified shall come into the world.
>
> And behold, I am the light and the life of the world; and I have

drunk out of that bitter cup which the Father hath given me, and have glorified the Father in taking upon me the sins of the world, in the which I have suffered the will of the Father in all things from the beginning. (11:10–11)

Pause just a moment on that last verse, where the Savior further describes himself and his mission. Three times he alludes to the Father, stressing repeatedly that he does the Father's will and he glorifies the Father. I ask you to notice how frequently this obedient Son speaks of his Father, and to his Father, during his ministry among the Lehite people. Except when he is delivering essentially the same sermon we now call the Sermon on the Mount, the Savior refers and defers countless times to his divine Father. The respect and obedience he shows to the Father is an unforgettable lesson for us.

The amazed multitude fall to the earth, but it is in seeing and feeling the nail prints in the Savior's hands, feet, and side that they know their Lord has come, as was prophesied. Overwhelmed, they cry out "Hosanna! Blessed be the name of the Most High God! And they did fall down at the feet of Jesus, and did worship him" (11:17). Their grief has turned to joy and thanksgiving.

Jesus immediately begins teaching, calling Nephi forward and giving him and others power to baptize. (He calls twelve disciples, just as he had in the Holy Land. See 3 Nephi 12:1.) His first instruction is about baptism, the manner of its performance and the specific words to be spoken. That Jesus addresses this matter before taking up other things is a sure indication of the extreme importance of the ordinance. He emphatically insists on baptism and the way it is to be conducted. At the same time, he virtually commands, as his doctrine, that all contention, over baptism procedures and anything else, "be done away" (11:30). The pure love that must prevail among his people cannot coexist with contention.

It is not my purpose to rehearse chapter by chapter the specific teachings of Jesus throughout the remainder of 3 Nephi. Others, and I myself, have discussed these teachings elsewhere. I must mention, however, that in repeating the principles he taught in the Sermon on the Mount, Jesus stresses again such attributes as humility, meekness, mercifulness, purity of heart, and peacemaking (see 3 Nephi 12:3–9). He also enjoins these people to come to him "with a broken heart and a contrite spirit" (12:19) and counsels them to "agree with thine adversary quickly" and not to "resist evil" (or seek vengeance), but to turn the other cheek, to walk away from evil (12:25, 39). Jesus seems to define the very essence of charity when he commands his listeners to "love your enemies, bless them that curse you, do good to them that hate you, and pray for them who despitefully use you and persecute you." For this is how to "be the children of your Father who is in heaven" (12:44–45). It is how Ammon and his brothers won the hearts and minds of their enemies, and how those repentant Lamanites won the hearts of some of their murderous kinsmen.

Having said that, I invite you to revisit with me the incredible scenes of his personal interactions with these repentant Saints and to rejoice in the experiences described as we rejoiced in the transforming moments of miracles and grace described in Part Two of this volume. My purpose is to remind all of us what can happen when pride and selfishness are supplanted by the pure love of Christ—a love expressed by him, through him, toward him, and toward others. In this great love, this simple yet magnificent thing Mormon called charity, lies the greatest joy the children of God can experience in mortality. Indeed, is there anything lovelier than receiving Christ's love and returning it to him through giving it out again to the "least of these," our brothers and sisters?

Let us go now, by way of transition, to 3 Nephi 16 where Jesus shows particular concern that his words be diligently recorded, that latter-day Gentiles might have the truth and then take that truth in its fulness to the house of Israel. He commands that his own words be written, and he repeatedly cites the commands and intentions of the Father in regard to these things. I note particularly that the Savior foresees latter-day Gentiles rejecting "the fulness" of his gospel, and being "lifted up in the pride of their hearts above all nations, and above all the people of the whole earth" (3 Nephi 16:10). I fear this describes too many of us in the promised land only too well, even if most of us can't rightly be accused of some of the other evils Jesus lists. The kind of pride Jesus describes is, again, the antithesis of charity, and he sees it infecting our country in our time.

Chapter 17 of 3 Nephi is one of the most beautiful, moving chapters in all of scripture. In stunning simplicity and perfection the record captures the tenderness, the infinite sweetness of the moment when the risen Lord ministers personally to his stricken people. Perhaps he understands his people's suffering with even greater poignancy now, for he had just taken on himself the sorrows, sins, and suffering of every human being who ever lived or ever will live. Think of the effect the Atonement must have had on Christ himself. Surely we see that effect as he pours out his love, unfeigned and unrestrained—the pure and perfect love that only he can extend in its fullest manifestation. And yet it is there for us to feel and to take into our hearts and to try in all humility and earnestness to extend to our fellow beings. If we truly want to become like him, we must show forth love in all his purity of intent. In this chapter, we are also blessed to witness what can happen when the heavens open in response to the pure love of Christ expressed among mortals who have humbly, gratefully, come to know their Lord.

The chapter opens as Jesus concludes his first day of teaching and begins to take his leave. He knows these people are overwhelmed by what they have seen and heard, that they have not fully understood all the Father has instructed him to teach them. Tenderly, he tells them to go home and "ponder" his words, to pray to the Father for understanding and "prepare your minds for the morrow" when he will return (3 Nephi 17:3). But as he looks at them and sees their tears and the longing in their eyes, he knows they want "him to tarry a little longer with them" (17:5). He is so "filled with compassion" that he stays, calling for them to bring "any that are lame, or blind, or halt or maimed, or leprous, or that are withered, or that are deaf, or that are afflicted in any manner" (17:6–7), and he will heal them. He speaks again of the compassion and overwhelming mercy that he feels.

They bring forth all who are afflicted in any way, "and he did heal them every one" (17:9). Envision this scene as

> . . . they did all, both they who had been healed and they who were whole, bow down at his feet, and did worship him; and as many as could come for the multitude did kiss his feet, insomuch that they did bathe his feet with their tears. (17:10)

And this is only the beginning of perhaps the most tender series of events earth's people have ever witnessed. The Savior asks that the little children be brought to him, and when they are brought, he directs the multitude to kneel. Groaning inwardly, he tells the Father that he is "troubled because of the wickedness of the people of the house of Israel" (17:14). Then

> . . . he himself also knelt upon the earth; and behold he prayed unto the Father, and the things which he prayed cannot be written, and the multitude did bear record who heard him. (17:15)

Mortal language is simply inadequate to represent the words uttered by the Lord of Creation as he kneels before his divine Father. Those present record the following in an effort to describe the wondrous event:

> The eye hath never seen, neither hath the ear heard before, so great and marvelous things as we saw and heard Jesus speak unto the Father;
>
> And no tongue can speak, neither can there be written by any man, neither can the hearts of men conceive so great and marvelous things as we both saw and heard Jesus speak; and no one can conceive of the joy which filled our souls at the time we heard him pray for us unto the Father. (17:16–17)

How would it feel to hear Jesus Christ pray to the Father, on his knees, for you? To feel, in his very presence, the magnitude of his love? The ancient record keepers may be unable to reproduce the Savior's words in tangible form, but they are well able to recreate the feelings that overflowed inside them. Reading of this event today, all these centuries later, we ourselves are taken to that temple site in Bountiful, to a structure that remained standing through widespread chaos and destruction. We, too, weep for joy and, like the multitude, are "overcome" (17:18).

And we cannot miss the fact that the Savior himself is also overcome. When he speaks, bidding the multitude to rise and confessing that his own "joy is full," he weeps; "and the multitude bare record of it, and he took their little children, one by one, and blessed them, and prayed unto the Father for them. And when he had done this he wept again" and said to the multitude, "Behold your little ones" (17:19–23). These precious experiences seem to serve as a prelude to what would follow. The people

> . . . cast their eyes towards heaven, and they saw the heavens open, and they saw angels descending out of heaven as if it were in the midst of fire; and they came down and encircled those little ones

159

about, and they were encircled about with fire; and the angels did minister unto them. (17:24)

Try to visualize what these people, and especially the innocent little children, have experienced in the past few days. First, envision earthquakes and fissures, eruptions, floods, tempests, fires, destruction, and death of proportions not seen since the days of Noah. And then picture thick darkness amidst all the destruction and chaos, and frightened parents trying to calm and comfort their terrified children. Next, hear a voice from out of the darkness, saying that just as he has often gathered Israel, and desired to gather them, he will again gather them. Three days pass in total darkness, and suddenly, light and joy break forth. The Father speaks from the heavens, and the Son descends to teach and bless and then to weep with and for his suffering people. In response, angels descend from the opened heavens. It is almost more than the finite mind can grasp, and I am filled with awe at every reading. I simply must quote the final verse in chapter 17, for always, always, the faithful bear record:

> And the multitude did see and hear and bear record; and they know that their record is true for they all of them did see and hear, every man for himself; and they were in number about two thousand and five hundred souls; and they did consist of men, women, and children. (17:25)

I love that passage, the solemn, measured simplicity of it and its deep, resounding profundity. Consider the final clauses: "And they were in number about two thousand and five hundred souls; and they did consist of men, women, and children." Those simple statements force us to read slowly and deliberately, to absorb their full meaning one word at a time. Compare them with a statement like this, which denotes essentially the same thing but reaches only our eyes: "Twenty-five hundred people were there." Unlike that flat statement of fact, the Book of Mormon passage is written from the heart and it speaks directly to the heart, the very truth and emotion of it bearing such a powerful witness that only the stubbornly closed mind could call it invention. These people were there. I know it as I know my own name.

If there is a chapter to rival 3 Nephi 17 in sheer spiritual power, it might well be 3 Nephi 19. Like chapter 17, it fills the soul. We should note, however, the importance of chapter 18, for it is here that the

Redeemer introduces the emblems that symbolize his great atoning sacrifice. He has chosen to remain longer still, instructing his twelve chosen disciples on the precise requirements and meaning of this vital ordinance. He also instructs the multitude on the matter and manner of prayer, especially in their families, and on the importance of meeting "together oft" and forbidding none from their worship services. They are to welcome and pray for those whom they might once have "cast . . . out" (3 Nephi 18:18–23).

Thus, as I have suggested before, even on what could well have been his first brief visit to earth, the resurrected Jesus teaches charity and seems to suggest that in extending pure love to others we arm ourselves against temptation (see 3 Nephi 18:25). Ready now to depart, he touches each of the twelve, speaking to them one by one, out of the hearing of the multitude, giving "them power to give the Holy Ghost" (18:36–37). Having done that, he ascends into heaven—a sacred event witnessed and borne record of only by the disciples.

You can imagine the buzz that traveled through Nephite lands among the survivors of the great upheaval. Learning that Jesus will return the next day, people labor through the night to get to him. So many come that they have to be divided into twelve bodies in order to receive instruction from the disciples. They are told to kneel and "pray unto the Father in the name of Jesus" (3 Nephi 19:6, 8). The disciples teach the words of Jesus and then kneel again and pray "for that which they most desired; . . . that the Holy Ghost should be given unto them" (19:9). It is when Nephi goes down into the water and baptizes the twelve that the miracles resume. I can feel the wonder in my very bones.

> The Holy Ghost did fall upon [the disciples], and they were filled with the Holy Ghost and with fire.
>
> And behold, they were encircled about as if it were by fire; and it came down from heaven, and the multitude did witness it, and did bear record; and angels did come down out of heaven and did minister unto them. (19:13–14)

This passage is just the beginning of still more events that defy description, for "while the angels were ministering unto the disciples, behold, Jesus came and stood in the midst and ministered unto them" (19:15). Immediately the resurrected Savior instructs the multitude and the disciples to kneel, commanding the latter to pray. And because he is present, they pray to him (see 19:22). Then he himself "went a little way off from them and bowed himself to the earth," thanking the Father for bestowing the Holy Ghost upon his chosen disciples. He then asks that the Father bestow that same gift on "all them that shall believe in their words" (19:19–21). Jesus teaches us here that he is not the ultimate source of the gift of the Holy Ghost. That priceless gift comes from the Father. Jesus concludes his prayer, but the disciples continue theirs, being "given . . . what they should pray, and they were filled with desire" (19:24). These words contain yet another lesson for us, this time on how we might approach our own prayers, sometimes waiting to be "given" what we should pray of and for.

Jesus then blesses his disciples as they pray, and they literally shine with his glory:

> His countenance did smile upon them, and the light of his countenance did shine upon them, and behold they were as white as the countenance and also the garments of Jesus; and behold the whiteness thereof did exceed all the whiteness, yea, even there could be nothing upon earth so white as the whiteness thereof. (19:25)

Five times in those few lines, the record repeats the word "white" or "whiteness" in an effort to describe a glory approaching the indescribable.

Again Jesus separates himself and prays for both the disciples and all others who will believe what they teach. The record reports that subsequently "he did smile upon [the disciples] again; and behold they were white, even as Jesus" (19:30). A third time, Jesus separates himself to pray to his Father in heaven, in words beyond earthly transcription:

> And tongue cannot speak the words which he prayed, neither can be written by man the words which he prayed.
>
> And the multitude did hear and do bear record; and their hearts were open and they did understand in their hearts the words which he prayed.
>
> Nevertheless, so great and marvelous were the words which he prayed that they cannot be written, neither can they be uttered by man. (19:32–34)

What must it have been like to be there—there where Christ's outpouring of love was almost tangible? Even though we can attend such an event only in our minds and hearts, we can take a great lesson from it. Some understandings only come through opening the mind and soul to holy, immortal speech.

And then Jesus makes a remarkable statement, avowing to his disciples that he has "never seen" such "great faith . . . among all the Jews"; consequently, "none of them . . . have seen so great things as ye have seen; neither have they heard so great things as ye have heard" (19:35–36). His teachings in the New World exceed those of his earthly ministry in the Holy Land. Readiness to receive is everything.

Chapters 20 through 27 of 3 Nephi consist of the Savior's further teachings and ministerings among the Nephite people, with major portions given to the scriptural teachings of Old Testament prophets. Included in these teachings, in addition to promises for the covenant people of Israel, are words of warning to the Gentiles, should they (we) prove unworthy of inheriting the promised land. But there are wondrous occurrences too. One of them is reported quite matter-of-factly in chapter 20, but it is anything but ordinary. It is the feeding of the multitude, a second time, in a manner similar to that described in the New Testament. First, Jesus breaks bread, blesses it, and gives it "to the disciples to eat." Next, he commands them to "break bread, and give unto the multitude"; then he provides wine, first for the disciples and next for the multitude (3 Nephi 20:3–5).

Jesus had done this on the first day of his appearance, when instituting the sacramental ordinance (see 3 Nephi 18:1–9). But when he returns the second day, thousands more have gathered. Mormon makes special note of the miracle—that "there had been no bread, neither wine, brought by the disciples, neither by the multitude." Nonetheless, "he truly gave unto them bread to eat, and also wine to drink," with an admonition and promise that we should never forget: "He that eateth this bread eateth of my body to his soul; and he that drinketh of this wine drinketh of my blood to his soul; and his soul shall never hunger nor thirst, but shall be filled" (20:6–8).

The physical feeding is representative not only of the Savior's atoning sacrifice and his role as the bread of life, but also of his spiritual feeding of these people. All three are expressions of his immeasurable love. It is a splendid moment, for "when the multitude had all eaten and drunk, behold, they were filled with the Spirit; and they did cry out with one voice, and gave glory to Jesus, whom they both saw and heard" (20:9). How much is contained in that one phrase, "whom they both saw and heard."

Mormon recounts at some length the Savior's decisive and repeated instructions and warnings about the record to come forth through a latter-day prophet (see chapters 21–25).[1] He informs us that on this occasion Jesus stayed and taught for "three days; and after that he did show himself unto them oft, and did break bread oft, and bless it, and give it unto them" (3 Nephi 26:13). The resurrected Christ personally and frequently strengthens and blesses these stricken people through the trials of rebuilding their cities and their lives. We are given just a brief sketch of what transpired in those visits, but the little we have suggests miracles without number. For example, this is what we learn of the miracles evinced through the children as Jesus ministers to them on the second day:

> He did loose their tongues, and they did speak unto their fathers great and marvelous things, even greater than he had revealed unto the people; and he loosed their tongues that they could utter. (26:14)

Mormon interrupts to remind us of the wondrous healings Jesus performed on the first day—healings such as giving sight to the blind and hearing to the deaf, and even raising "a man from the dead" (26:15). But then, Mormon returns to the children, whom the multitude "both saw and heard." He continues,

> Yea, even babes did open their mouths and utter marvelous things; and the things which they did utter were forbidden that there should not any man write them. (26:16).

What an experience that must have been, to hear such utterances from the mouths of little children, even tiny babes. I suspect that their spirit selves were given voice.

---

1. Chapter 21 is especially important to our day because Jesus speaks earnestly and repeatedly of the time when his words and promises to these ancient people (written in the record and brought forth through his "servant"—clearly Joseph Smith) will be made known. That occurrence will signify that "a great and a marvelous work" of the Father (3 Nephi 21:9, 10) has commenced in the last days. I find it interesting that the first seven verses of this chapter are presented as one single sentence. They are linked by the phrase "these things," or "these works," a phrase which appears in six of the seven verses. In verse 6, the pronoun "it" refers to the record, just as "these things" and "these works" refer to it in the other verses. The record, clearly, is of the utmost importance.

Rich blessings continue to flow, and miracles do not cease as the disciples go forth teaching and baptizing. "Filled with the Holy Ghost," many of these spiritually renewed people "saw and heard unspeakable things, which are not lawful to be written." More lovely still, "they taught, and did minister one to another; and they had all things common among them, every man dealing justly, one with another" (26:17–19). The ideal of charity lived at the waters of Mormon has been reborn with the Savior's arrival, and with his healings and teachings, after the great cleansing. That ideal sets a standard for us.

In chapter 27 of 3 Nephi, Jesus defines for his disciples just what his gospel is, repeatedly using the phrase "my gospel" and describing it in terms of his appointed mission and the judgment that awaits all of us. Repentance, baptism, and reception of the Holy Ghost are required of us, and more. "The works which ye have seen me do," he says, "shall ye also do" (3 Nephi 27:21). Those works, we remember, are works of healing, blessing, and teaching. Works of love, all of them. The Savior rejoices because none of this generation of Nephites who survived the cataclysm "are lost; and in them," he says, "I have fulness of joy" (27:31). Sadly, however, he foresees that "the fourth generation from this generation" will succumb to the devil's lures and become his captives. "They will sell me for silver and for gold, and for that which moth doth corrupt and which thieves can break through and steal" (27:32). In other words, they will become worldly, selfish, greedy, and prideful. They will no longer embrace the pure love of Christ.

The final chapter chronicling the Savior's work among the Nephites is 3 Nephi 28. It depicts the miraculous transformation of three selfless Nephite disciples who have asked to remain on earth, teaching and bringing souls to Christ until he returns in glory to initiate a millennium of peace. Knowing their righteous thoughts, their desire for "the thing which John, my beloved . . . desired of me" (3 Nephi 28:6), Jesus grants their wish. They will not taste of death, nor will they experience physical pain, though evil people will try to harm them. Just before he departs, Jesus touches the disciples with his finger, but he does not touch the three. When he leaves, "the heavens were opened, and they were caught up into heaven, and saw and heard unspeakable things," things they were forbidden to utter. Significantly, the power to "utter the things which they saw and heard" (28:14) is withheld from them.

Mormon doesn't learn the precise nature of the change in their bodies until later (see 3 Nephi 28:36–40), but he reports their initial response to the miracle wrought in their persons:

> And whether they were in the body or out of the body, they could not tell; for it did seem unto them like a transfiguration of them, that they were changed from this body of flesh into an immortal state, that they could behold the things of God. (28:15)

We are allowed only brief glimpses into the miracle-filled early ministry of these blessed three as they go forth teaching under the protecting care of heaven. Leaving the refuge of Nephite church members, they "go forth upon the face of the land, and . . . minister unto all the people, uniting as many to the church as would believe in their preaching; baptizing them, and as many as were baptized did receive the Holy Ghost" (28:18). Their whole purpose is to serve others and bring them to truth and ultimate redemption. We are reminded of earlier Nephite teachers who had gone forth with the same purpose.

The reception of the three among the larger populace is often anything but pleasant and fruitful. They are "cast into prison," "cast down into the earth," "thrice . . . cast into a furnace," and "twice . . . cast into a den of wild beasts." Miracles abound, however: "prisons could not hold them, for they were rent in twain"; pits could not hold them, for "they did smite the earth with the word of God," and "were delivered." Likewise, they "received no harm" from the furnace, and they "did play with the beasts as a child with a suckling lamb, and received no harm" (28:19–22).

Every one of these instances holds a story of its own, a story of wondrous rescue of the Lord's loving and divinely protected servants. Maybe one day you and I will read those stories. After all, Mormon promised just pages earlier that "when they [you and I] shall have received this [the abridged record], which is expedient that they should have first, to try their faith, and if it shall so be that they shall believe these things then shall the greater things be made manifest unto them" (3 Nephi 26:9). "The greater things" Mormon speaks of are presumably in the sealed portion of the record.

Mormon is forbidden to write the names of the three who are allowed to remain, but he makes a stunning personal statement before giving a quick summary of their mission. He says, "But behold, *I have seen them, and they have ministered unto me*" (3 Nephi 28:26, emphasis added). Mormon, four centuries later, has been strengthened and blessed by these men, as has his son Moroni (see Mormon 8:11). Mormon compares them to "the angels of God," performing "great and marvelous works," even "among the Gentiles" (28:27–31). Truly, these disciples are men of immense charity, men of the purest kind of love, whose work stretches endlessly through the ages until the Second Coming of the Lord who called them.

So ends the abridged account of Christ's ministry among his people in the New World, in the meridian of time. And a glorious account it is. Again, I am aware of my immense debt to my Savior; to his prophets of old who faithfully, and at great personal cost, kept the record we call the Book of Mormon; to the record's selfless and inspired translator, Joseph Smith; and to the Lord's devoted, loving prophets today who teach and live by its precepts. And then, there are Mormon and his son Moroni, whose lives of pure love are engraved into every page I am blessed to read and ponder. My gratitude is beyond mortal words to express. I am ever thankful that the Lord can read my heart, and I long to reach the point where I am beyond selfishness, beyond pride, beyond unkindness, beyond worldliness. Child of the world though I too often am, I long to become the person I should be. I long to embrace and extend, with my whole being, the pure love of Christ. Charity.

ABOUT THE *Author*

An Emeritus Professor of English at Brigham Young University, Marilyn Arnold served as Assistant to the President under Dallin H. Oaks and Dean of Graduate Studies under Jeffrey R. Holland.

A nationally known literary scholar, she has published widely in the academic world, as well as in Church publications. She has also lectured and led discussions on the Book of Mormon in many settings, most recently on "Hugh Nibley on the Book of Mormon" at the BYU Nibley Centennial lecture series (2010) and the St. George tabernacle. She will deliver the fifth annual Neal A. Maxwell lecture at BYU in 2011, on the Book of Mormon and discipleship.

Her classic work on the Book of Mormon, *Sweet Is the Word: Reflections on the Book of Mormon*, is well-known in Mormondom. Another destined classic is *Sacred Hymns of the Book of Mormon*, a collection of thirty-two original hymns, for which she wrote the lyrics and Maurine Ozment composed the music. Marilyn also served as an associate editor for the massive *Book of Mormon Reference Companion*, and on the editorial board for the *Journal of Book of Mormon Studies*. She has authored eight published novels—one of them a national award winner—and several books of non-fiction, including *Bittersweet: A Daughter's Memoir* (2010). In 2003 she was honored as a Woman of Achievement by the state of Utah in a special ceremony at the Capitol. In 2006 she received the Distinguished Citizen award from Dixie State College.